SHADES
OF LIGHT

For Nick, Rachel and George

SHADES OF LIGHT

MAKING TAILORED LAMPSHADES

Ruth De Fraga Gomes

ROBERT HALE • LONDON

ISBN 978-0-7198-1105-0

Robert Hale Limited
Clerkenwell House
Clerkenwell Green
London EC1R 0HT

www.halebooks.com

A catalogue record for this book is available from the British Library

10 9 8 7 6 5 4 3 2 1

Typeset by Eurodesign
Printed in Singapore

Contents

Preface

I have been making lampshades over the past fifteen years and run a small business doing so from a workshop at the bottom of my garden. Having originally come from a fashion background this craft has enabled me to develop my interest in fabric, colour, design, trim and embellishment whilst affording me the flexibility to bring up a family. For the past seven years I have also taught traditional lampshade making to small groups in creative studios and colleges and, along with my own experience, this has given me the depth of knowledge that an instructional book requires. I have hopefully experienced, or seen through my students, every pitfall, frustration and commonly made mistake, and worked out a way to get round each of these potential disasters! I hope to pass on all of these 'wrinkles' to you in the hope that you are successful in your own projects and able to enjoy the craft as much as I do.

Traditional lampshade making doesn't need a large financial outlay and is a flexible craft. You only need a small space to work in and some parts of the process are portable; they can be done on your lap or when sitting out in the garden. There is little specialist equipment to have to buy, most equipment required being found in a basic sewing kit, and not a lot of fabric is required, so remnants can be used. Fabrics that are suitable are usually of a dress weight, so even clothes can be taken apart and re-fashioned into a tailored cover. It is worth hunting in charity shops, junk shops, house clearances and car boot sales for old lampshades to strip down and re-cover. There can be a large element of recycling involved and minimal cost. Try to use what you have.

This is not a glossy coffee table book full of photographs with beautifully styled rooms; it is a 'how to' book so there is plenty of written instruction. This gives you the skills to make the shade properly, in the traditional way, and really not a lot has changed since they were first made in the nineteenth century. By discovering the advantages

and limitations of a traditionally hand-crafted shade you can start to design them yourself and, whether that is to do with choice of colour, shape of frame or particular embellishment, you can really make them your own. I have taught florists who bring to the craft their knowledge of colour and struc-

ture, milliners who love to embellish with hat-inspired trimmings such as feathers and corsages, dressmakers who take inspiration from clothing shapes and dressmaking techniques. This is the starting point. Read it carefully, and stick with it; it works, I've tested it!

Acknowledgements

Many thanks to all the people who have helped me with this book. To Millie Sewell Knight for the illustrations, to Craig Cole, Reed's School studio photography club, Scott Lewis and Rachel De Fraga Gomes for the photographs and to Sandra Thompson and Emma Wilkinson for making some of the shades. Thank you to all of my friends and family who have been so supportive, but special thanks to my husband Nick and to Rachel and George for giving me the space to write this book, general encouragement and delivering endless cups of tea to my workshop!

Introduction and History

*L*ampshades are covered frames that fit onto the top of a lamp, cover the lighting source and diffuse the light that is being emitted. They serve both a decorative and practical purpose and can be made of paper, velum, glass, card, plastic, parchment and many other materials. However, this book explores the traditional tailored lampshade that is made of fabric stretched over a frame. The fabric shade's history, construction and design will be covered, showing the traditional methods which have changed very little over the years, since they were first introduced. Even if traditional methods of making are used, lampshades need not look traditional and old-fashioned, indeed sometimes the traditional methods of making allow for more ambitious modern designs to be produced. This book looks at design, trends and embellishment as well as the practical skills required.

Fabric lampshades were first used on oil lamps in the home. Most shades at this time were made of glass; however silk shades did start to appear alongside them. They were introduced amidst concerns about damage to eyesight from the glare of the flame. The silk shade obviously had to be protected from the naked flame in the oil burner, and this was achieved by a simple interior protective globe or tube. These protective cylinders were made of glass or mica and prevented the fabric catching fire. Count Rumford advised: 'Screens composed of such a substance as disperse the light without destroying it. Ground glass, thin white silk stuffs may be used for that purpose …' And so the silk shade was born.

A major breakthrough in increasing the brightness of the oil burner was made when the incandescent mantle was introduced in 1893. These mantles were used for both oil and gas lights. They consisted of a silk or cotton knitted fabric impregnated with a mixture of chemical salts. The mantle was suspended in the flame of an oil or gas lamp and when it reached a certain temperature it produced a bright white light about twelve times as great as that emitted by a flat flame burner. This is when the lampshade became a necessity: shades were used as the light emitted from this gas lighting, a harsh, bright white light, was simply too bright for the eyes and considered to be unflattering. J.G. Lockhart noted:

183

HINKS' LAMPS

SILK SHADES

494
Figured Silk, with Green Bead Fringe.
20 in. ... 26/3

457
Empire, Jap. Silk, Lined White.
Trimmed with Best Chiffon Ribbon, and Bead Fringe.
20 in. ... 25/6

485
Florentine Silk.
18 in. ... 14/3

465
Empire, Florentine Silk and Bead Fringe.
15 in. ... 17/-

481
Handkerchief Shade.
Rich Embroidered Chiffon over Silk, with Bead Fringe.
15 in. ... 24/-
Made in Three Colours only, viz.:
Nil, Vieux Rose, and Gold.

469
Florentine Silk, Chiffon and Silk Flounce.
Trimmed with Chiffon Ribbon and Lace Insertion.
18 in. ... 30/-
20 in. ... 33/9

HINKS' LAMPS

SILK SHADES.

449
Florentine Silk and Best Lace.
20 in. ... 29/3

489
Florentine Silk.
18 in. ... 30/9
20 in. ... 33/9

490
Florentine Silk.
18 in. ... 31/6
20 in. ... 34/6

454
Florentine Silk and Fancy Chiffon, with Bead Fringe.
18 in. ... 32/3

475
Fancy Chiffon, Lined with Florentine Silk, and
Deep Puffed Chiffon Flounce.
20 in. ... 35/3

468
Florentine Silk, Puffed Shaded Chiffon Flounce.
18 in. ... 36/-
20 in. ... 39/-

'Suddenly at the turning of a screw, the room was filled with a gush of splendour, worthy of a Palace of Aladdin … jewellery sparkled, but cheeks and lips looked pale and wan in this illumination, and the eye was wearied and the brows ached if the sitting was at all protracted.'

So the shades filtered and diffused this intense light. Initially they were mostly made of opal glass, but gradually the shade made of fabric stretched over a wire frame started to become popular because it could be so decorative, and the silk lampshade became the norm in most homes.

The popularity of the fabric lampshade increased further with the development of the electric light bulb in the late nineteenth century. Joseph Swan and Thomas Edison developed this filament electric light bulb independently, the great advantage of this being the absence of the naked flame. Fabric shades could now be used relatively safely without the need for the glass safety shield. This said, although silk shades were popular during this time, glass shades were still preferred in America and France.

The primary focus during this first era of domestic lighting was for lamps to give a good level of illumination in the home. However, during the following Victorian period the emphasis seemed to be on creating a mood or ambiance rather than the room being brightly lit. In fact a lot of Victorian rooms were

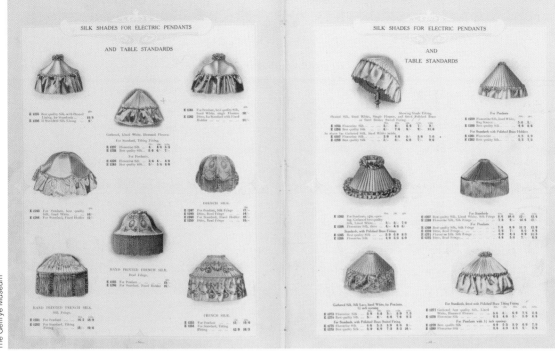

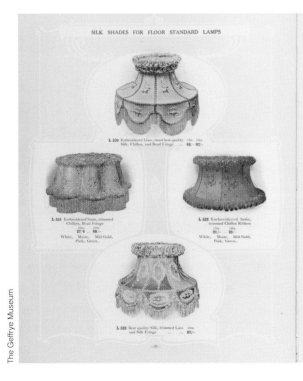

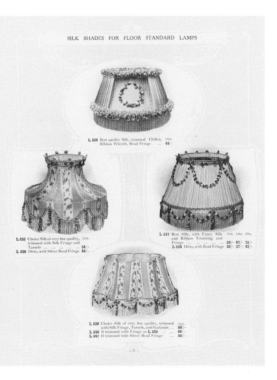

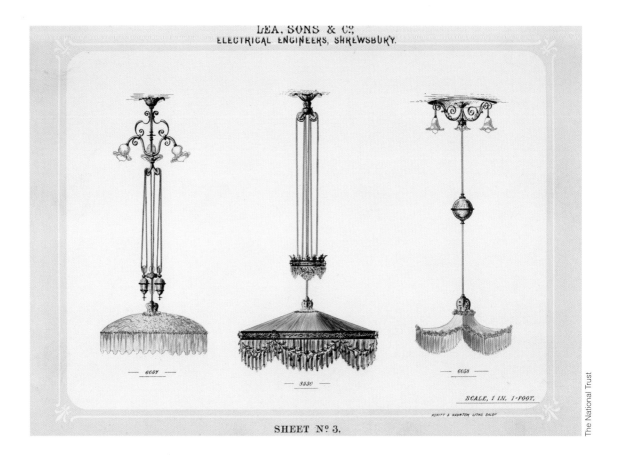

LEA, SONS & Cº

ELECTRICAL ENGINEERS, SHREWSBURY.

— 6067 —

— 8580 —

— 6058 —

SCALE, 1 IN. 1-FOOT.

ASHITY & NAUNTON LITHS. SALOP

SHEET Nº 3.

quite gloomy; possibly on account of the very heavily decorated lampshades that allowed little light into the room. These first decorative lampshades were very reminiscent of the dresses and hats that were the fashion of the period. They were usually made of silk and typically very ornate. They were pleated, gathered and ruched and heavily trimmed with swags, frills, tassels, ribbons and lace, often on fluted and scalloped galleried frame edges. Some of the standard lamps had large shades decorated with bows, layers of lace and artificial leaves and flowers. As a result of these many layers of fabric and decoration, not much light was actually emitted through the shade, so the lighting effect was somewhat dismal. In the early 1890s this new fashion in shade design was described by Aymer Vallance in the *Art Journal*: 'Unhappily it is the fashion to use elaborate shades of silk or lace or ribbons or of crimped paper ruched like a lady's skirt. Such things savour too much of Parisian millinery and moreover are liable, if left for any length of time unwatched, to become scorched and catch fire.'

An additional problem with these decorative shades was that the layers of fabric, artificial foliage and flowers

made these shades very attractive to spiders, so small nets called spider screens had to be fixed inside the shade in an attempt to deter them.

Even small silk shades that were used on wall sconces or on chandeliers were often just as elaborate and the demand for all these shades became so great that in 1901 the firm of James Hinks and Sons was reported to have 'a large factory solely devoted to turning out these shades'.

During the Edwardian period the shades were still very elaborate, but tended to have bead and silk fringing instead of the intricate lace, flounces and frills. At Arkington Court Mr Newman recalled 'wonderful Edwardian lampshades like big hats in pink silk with lace fringes kept in boxes and used on standard lamps'.

Art Nouveau and Art Deco lampshades dominated the period between 1920 and 1930 and the emphasis moved from fabric shades to glass. This was really the era of the glass shade, in particular the Tiffany shade, although other materials such as mock vellum, parchment and early forms of plastic were being used. There were, however, some fabric shades around and these were often hand-painted with elaborate flowers and birds – particularly parrots. They tended to be trimmed with long chainette fringing, bead fringing and tassels. The shades were often made in simple panelled shapes that were sewn at home.

The National Trust

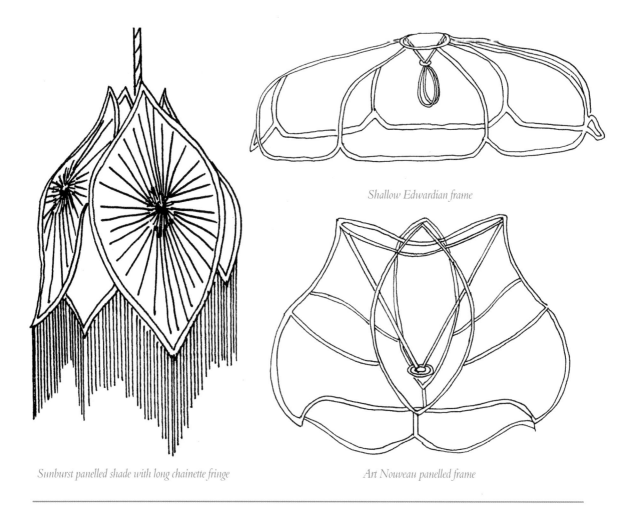

Shallow Edwardian frame

Sunburst panelled shade with long chainette fringe

Art Nouveau panelled frame

This era also gave rise to the chiffon sunburst panelled shade, the sunburst being a popular Art Deco motif of the time, and also shades became shallower than their Edwardian predecessors. This was the first time that an asymmetric element was introduced to their design, some frames having an asymmetric bottom ring.

In her 1921 book *Lampshades – How to Make Them*, Olive Earle says:

The purpose of this book is to make the art of shading lamps and candles a little less of a problem to the amateur craftsman; and it is hoped, also, that those who have already had some experience as shade makers, will find some practical hints that will be of value to them. Miss M. L. Morey, who is well known as a designer and maker of lampshades, has given me the solution to many of the problems that beset the beginner.

Not all shades were made at home and notable designers and manufacturers making fabric shades at this time were W.A.S. Benson (1854–1924), who made silk shades with flounces, Dufreine Maurice (1876–1955), who produced netted silk and taffeta shades with silk tassels, and Subes Raymon (1893–1970). In the early 1920s the last-named had a Madame Lehuche-Mery make a range of embroidered shades for his company.

The period between the 1940s and 1950s saw chiffon pleating and swathing being used extensively. As fabric was rationed, parachute silk was used to make shades, and tailored and kitchen lampshades started to be made out of re-fashioned clothing and utility fabrics. Books even showed readers how to make their own frames.

In her 1953 publication *Lampshade Making – Book Number Two* F.J. Christopher wrote:

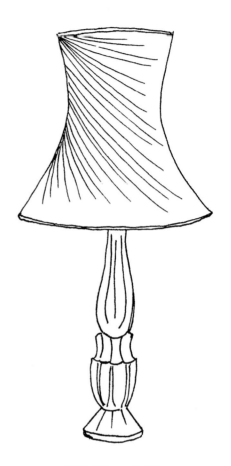

1940s chiffon swathed shade

Thousands of people are now making lampshades at home for a variety of reasons, which embrace the high cost of shop-bought shades, the urge to some useful form of handiwork and the need to supplement slender incomes. Whatever the reason for the present great interest in lampshade making, there is no doubt that it is one of the pleasantest of all home occupations. The materials are not costly, the work is clean and light, and the finished products amply recompense the worker for the cost of materials and the time expended.

The 1960s shades employed a lot of the fabrics and techniques fashionable at the time. Terylene, nylons, rayons, voile and nylon nets were used extensively, as was the technique of smocking. Care had to be taken with these shades as the synthetic fabrics had a tendency to melt rather than scorch if they were too close to the bulb.

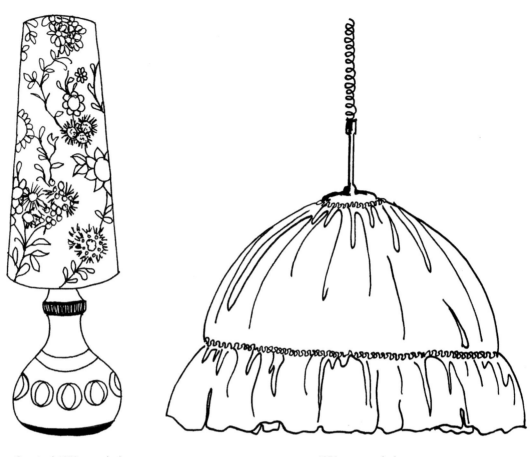

Oversized 1970s cone shade   *1970s mop cap shade*

Oversized cones or dunce shades were popular in the 1970s, the standard lamp being replaced by large ceramic bases with tall cone shades standing up to 1.5m high. These shades were often made in textured fabrics, slub linens and brightly printed cottons of the time. The 1970s also saw the Tiffany-shaped pendant light, often with a mop cap shade or tailored with long chainette fringing.

The coolie shade became very popular in the 1980s and shades were often decorated with lots of ruffles and frills. Knife-pleated and box-pleated shades were fashionable, as well as lots of surface decoration such as faux swags. The fashion for matching all of the soft furnishings in the room meant that lampshades were often made of the same fabric as that of the curtains, loose covers, cushions and bed linens. The 1990s continued this decorative trend: shades had lots of heavy tasselling and fringing. Traditional shapes were popular, particularly the bowed empire and galleried shades.

The turn of the century saw lampshades having a much cleaner minimalist look, shallow bowed drums, true drums and asymmetric shapes, the emphasis here being on the shape rather than any surface decoration. This is also where the kitchen shade became popular again. A resurgence of interest in 'make do and mend' and general home crafts encouraged people to make their own shades and the kitchen shade was a good starting point. The rise of the 'vintage' market helped increase interest in old shades and 'upcycling'.

From 2010 onwards the trends include hanging clusters of shades in different shapes and sizes and at different heights, but from a central point, and also naked skeleton shades where the frame itself is the feature. The frame isn't covered at all, but sometimes it is bound with decorative tape and adorned with brooches, corsages, ribbons, etc. This type of 'shade' (if it can be called that, as it doesn't shade the eyes from the glare of the light bulb) has become popular as the dimmer switch has become widely used. Half-covered or old 'distressed' shades are also fashionable and many retailers have hung lots of different pendant shades around their shops, with the emphasis being on an interesting lining rather than the outer tailored cover. Chiffon swathing and panelled sunray shades are now often used by stylists in fashion magazines and as such are becoming popular.

Interior styling often follows fashion trends and lampshades are a part of this. New fabric technologies, a different emphasis on silhouette, colour trends and embellishment all help to form our ideas of what is fashionable but, throughout the ages, the actual traditional construction of a lampshade has remained the same.

Hanging cluster shades

CHAPTER ONE

Function

W hen designing a lampshade, it is important to know what its function
is. Shades are often an afterthought in a design scheme which is a
shame as, although they are decorative, they do form part of the room's
lighting requirement.

Lighting falls into four main categories, ambient, task or reading, accent and feature. These categories are not mutually exclusive and shades often fulfil two or more of these functions in any lighting scheme.

Ambient lighting

Ambient lighting is general room illumination. It is background lighting, not directed at anything in particular and makes up for any lack of natural daylight in a room. It can also add warmth to a large space and can be provided by a combination of different light sources around the room that form overlapping pools of light such as wall sconces, pendant, table and standard lamps. The higher the shade is from the floor on a standard lamp, the broader the spill of light into the room. Standard lampshades tend to be large, and their large, open top rings can throw light upwards, which then 'bounces' off the ceiling into the room.

Task or reading lighting

Task or reading lighting is directed, focused light that creates a bright spot that either highlights something or creates bright lighting for a work table or for an activity such as reading or sewing. The first requirement of a shade in this situation is that it needs to be big enough to accommodate a high-wattage bulb. The smaller the shade, the less wattage you can use because of the heat emitted from the bulb (although the new low-wattage bulbs are now much cooler). Secondly a shade for task lighting ideally needs to have a small-diameter top ring and wider bottom ring in order to focus the light downwards. Table and floor lamps situated correctly and with the right shades can provide this bright, focused light and lamps with long flexible arms and heads are perfect for this function. Even a low-hanging pendant light over a kitchen table will provide a task light for preparing food.

Accent lighting

Accent lighting is soft, indirect lighting and is often used for lighting a dark corner of a room or to throw a soft light on a dressing table or console table. It can be used for aesthetics and safety and, unlike task lighting, lights up an area to enhance it rather than pointing a specific light at it. Most shades fulfil this purpose successfully. However, shades that have top and bottom rings of a similar diameter work particularly well as they don't direct light in any one direction. They emit their light both up and down and through the fabric of the shade.

Drums, bowed drums, canister drums, empires and bowed empires with large-diameter top rings are ideal frame shapes.

Feature lighting

Feature lighting is where the lamp's function is primarily decorative; a piece of decorative art that can be illuminated. A lamp has, of course, to be functional so to some extent it can supplement a room's ambient lighting, but the lighting aspect of feature lighting is secondary to the aesthetic. Lampshades in this category can be very slim as they don't have to accommodate a large bulb; they can be heavily embellished as there is no need for a lot of light to be emitted through the body of the shade and they can be an interesting shape as there is no need to throw light in a particular direction. These lamps display light as an art-form.

CHAPTER TWO

Proportion

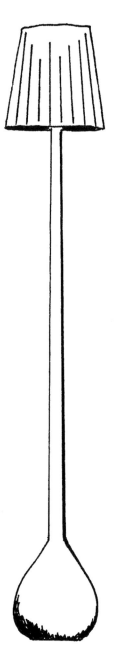

T here are no hard and fast rules when it comes to the proportion of the shade to the base – to some extent it comes down to whether you feel it looks right for the setting that the lamp is in, the style of the lamp and your own personal taste. When the proportion is wrong you, as a creative person, will tend just to know, as your eye is often drawn to it. So it is worth persevering with different shapes and sizes of shade to get it right. Have a critical eye and trust your instincts.

Personal taste and placement

If you are not having a frame made and are using frames you have already, then skeleton shades (those that are yet to be covered – i.e. the bare frame) are diffi-cult to use for this as you can see straight through them. It is worth roughly pegging a piece of fabric over the shade as if it were covered to help with the decision; this gives the shade some 'body' and it is easier to visualize.

Some people like their shades to sit low down, covering a lot of the base, whilst others prefer them to be teetering high on the base. As well as personal taste, a lot does depend on from where the lamp is primarily going to be

An example of a shade that is too small for the base

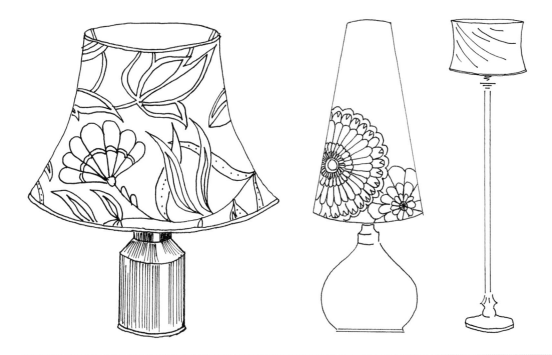

viewed. A shade on a lamp on a low coffee table, when standing and viewed from above, would look as though the shade was overwhelming the base, but as soon as you view it from a seated position, you will be viewing it from a completely different angle and height and it may appear acceptable.

The size of the shade may also have to be determined by space constraints. If it is too big, it could be knocked if it is in a busy thoroughfare and if it is too tall, for example, it may block a picture or wall mirror.

As well as the height and angle from which it is being viewed there are trends to consider. A tall, slender lamp base with a small shade gives a modern directional look, although it may break all the rules regarding proportion.

1970s style lamps with oversize tall cone shades and small bases also turn the proportions rule upside down but still appear to work. So it really is worth experimenting until you find what suits you and the setting.

Guiding principles

Having said all of this there are, however, a few basic principles that may be helpful when making your design decision.

- Your lampshade should not over-whelm the base of your lamp or look too top-heavy. If your shade is more than half of the height of the base the lamp is likely to look top-heavy.

Above left An example of a shade that is too large for the base

Above Examples of shade-to-base proportions that break the rules but still work. The 1970s cone shade is almost double the height of the base, yet works and is very reminiscent of the era. The small bowed drum on a very tall slim base should look too small but in fact looks minimalist and modern.

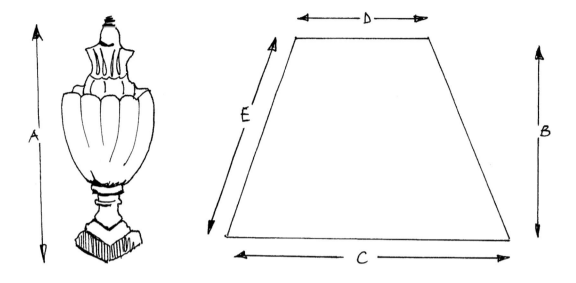

Diagram showing the five measurements to consider

- The shade should, however, cover the workings of the lamp, that is the light bulb, spindle and neck of the base. Ideally the lower edge of the shade should be about 5cm below the bottom of the bulb socket.
- For traditional shades, the base of the shade should always be wider than the width of the base. However, a shade that is too wide will take up a lot of space and, as mentioned before, risks being knocked. This is where a rectangular or oval shade may be more appropriate as it gives the width aesthetic without the depth.
- If you are really stuck, the following is a good rule of thumb if you want a traditional look and are working with a straight or bowed empire. There are five measurements to consider.

A Height of base
B* Height or 'drop' of shade
C Diameter of bottom ring
D Diameter of top ring
E Slope

B* If your shade is to have tassels, a beaded drop or fringe trim on the bottom ring, this will make the shade appear taller, so allow for this in your measurement of the drop or height.

- The diameter of the bottom ring of the shade should be approximately 80% of the height of the base.
- The diameter of the top ring should be approximately 50% of the diameter of the bottom ring.
- When the shade is on the base, it should form between 33% and 40% of the total height of the lamp and base.

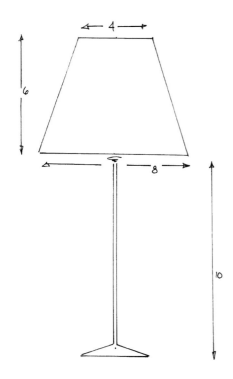

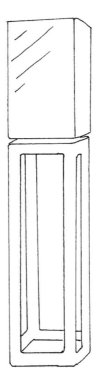

The shade and base of the lamp are of the same shape and complement each other perfectly

Far left *Diagram showing the rule of thumb for a perfectly proportioned shade-to-base ratio*

The shape and size of the shade should complement not only the room style, but the base itself. A good design rule is to have only one dominant element to the lamp; either the shade or the base. If the base is ornate, keep the shade simple, and vice versa. For example, an intricate hand-painted base needs a plain shade to highlight the base, whereas a highly embellished, patterned shade needs a plain base.

This can also apply to colour of base and shade. If the base and shade are to be of the same colour, keep the shapes of both relatively simple – less is more.

When thinking about the design of a shade, an element of the base can be

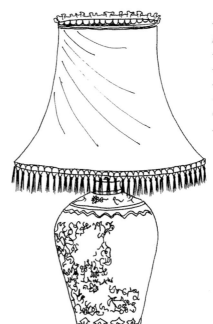

An ornate base and patterned embellished shade may work in some very traditional settings, but it is usually better to have either the base or the shade as the feature

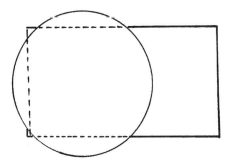 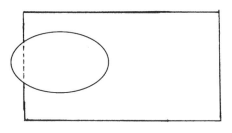

Arial view. An oval shade on a side table still gives the look of a curved drum shade without taking up as much space

reflected in some way in the design or embellishment of the shade. For a modern look, pair clean lines of the base and shade, and for a feature base such as an elephant base, a pagoda-style shade is fitting. Try to make sure that the shade and base complement each other rather than compete, not only in size and shape, but in embellishment colour and theme.

It is also sometimes fitting to echo the shape of the piece of furniture that the lamp is to be placed on, for example an oval shade on an oval table.

A useful practical exercise is to cut out of paper a scale drawing of the lamp base and experiment with different cut-out paper shades. These are easy to interchange and can be a useful tool in the design process.

Scott Lewis Photography

CHAPTER THREE

Elements of a Frame

Y ou will first need a lampshade frame. From a supplier these will usually be plastic coated (in white) but many frames that are found in charity shops and auctions (and indeed some that are specially made) will be uncoated, i.e. they will be in their natural metal state.

Sourcing and preparing frames

When buying a second-hand frame it is worth examining it to make sure it isn't distorted. It may have been stored for a long time or have been knocked or dropped during a house move. Stand it on a flat surface and see if it sits squarely and that all the struts are symmetrical. A distorted frame can cause all sorts of problems when making a tailored shade, so it is worth checking. It is also important to check that there are enough struts on the frame to use the traditional method of shade making. Often, if the shade was originally a firm shade made of card, the frame won't have enough struts because the card itself formed the shape and body of the shade. Fabric alone is unable to do this; it needs the struts to form the shape.

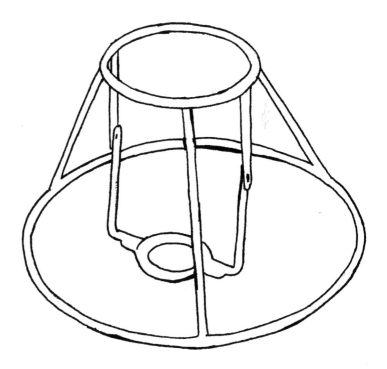

The frame from a card shade

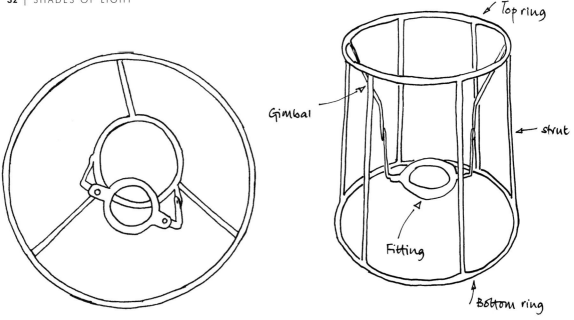

Top ring

Gimbal

strut

Fitting

Bottom ring

The illustration (above left) shows a frame whose shade was originally made of card, so only required three struts; using this to make a tailored shade would result in an odd triangular-shaped shade.

A bare metal frame either needs to be completely bound with straight frame tape (see Chapter 8 for more information on binding) or the frame can be spray-painted. If you have a lot of frames to be coated, it may be worth approaching a powder coating company. This plasticized coating is very durable, but expensive if done individually. If the frame is to be spray-painted, first rub off any rust with emery paper —shades can only be washed successfully if the frame is properly prepared as any rust will stain. Then prime the frame with spray primer and paint with spray paint. Car paint and spray enamel work well. Hang the frame outside on a washing line or free-standing hook and spray a couple of coats to give good coverage. This also gives you the opportunity to paint the frame in a complementary colour to the shade itself, giving a really bespoke look. This is particularly useful when making black shades as the white fitting and gimbals, which are visible after the shade has been made, are very obvious against black fabric.

Elements of a frame

The elements of a frame are shown in the diagram above. The top and bottom rings are always referred to as 'rings' even if they are square and the metal rods joining the top and bottom rings

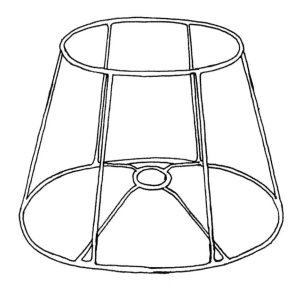

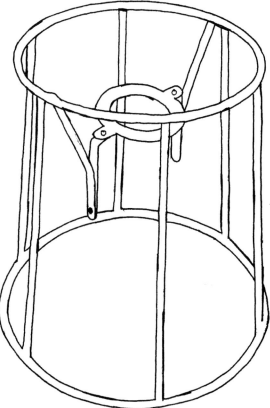

are the struts. The gimbal joins the fitting onto the frame and this gimbal can be fixed or reversible. The fitting is the part that fits around the light source and can vary in type and size.

Although there are usually two gimbals on a frame, larger frames often have three or four gimbals to give the frame stability. The gimbal can also be fixed on the bottom ring, especially with taller shades, where if the gimbals originated from the top ring, they would become too long and wobbly.

A reversible gimbal is one which has a join with a screw halfway along its length on which it can pivot. This allows for the shade to be used on a lamp base or when the gimbal is turned the other way, as a pendant shade (one that hangs from the ceiling). It also allows the shade to be 'cocked' at an angle like a hat to give a different look.

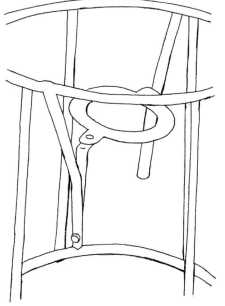

Above left *Frame with fixed gimbal from the bottom ring to give stability*

Above *Frame with gimbal reversed to make a pendant shade*

Left *Detail of reversible gimbal showing the pivot point*

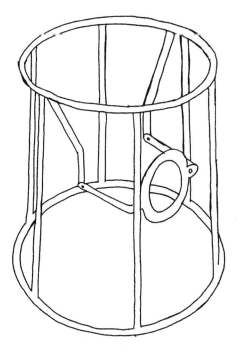

Frame with gimbal cocked at an angle

A reverse gimbal is used on this lampshade to 'cock' the shade to one side

Scott Lewis Photography

Frame fittings

The fitting of the frame is the means by which the shade fits onto the light source, whether that is a lamp base or a ceiling fitting. Fittings differ around the world; those commonly found on lamps in the UK are known as the standard British fitting, and now the European ES fitting is becoming much more wide-spread. A British fitting will accept a bulb stem with a diameter of 22mm whereas an ES fitting will accept a bulb stem with a diameter of 27mm. This larger aperture on the frame can be easily converted into a British fitting, by way of a small plastic converter which clips inside the ES ring fitting. Nowa-days this is an ideal fitting to have made as it can accommodate both lamp base fittings whereas the British fitting on a frame is much more limiting.

DUPLEX

The duplex fitting tends to be found on larger standard frames where stability is important and being large the frame has the space to accommodate this larger 110mm fitting. A duplex fitting is used with a shade carrier which is fixed to the lamp and the duplex fitting fits on top. This allows the shade to be used on both British and European fittings as the shade carriers which fix to the lamp base are available in both fittings.

Shade carriers are available in different heights, usually in increments of 2 to 3cm. This allows the shade to

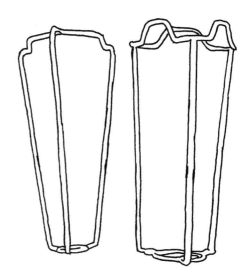

Frame with duplex fitting

Two types of shade carriers for a shade with a duplex fitting

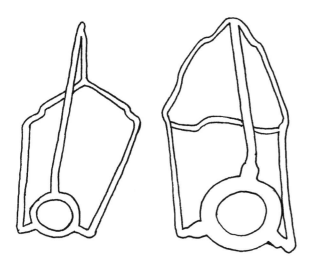

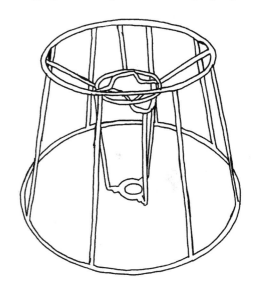

Shade carriers showing the smaller British and larger ES lamp fitting

The carrier is sited in the frame with the duplex fitting

be held on the lamp base at different heights. An incredibly useful and versatile fitting, but only suitable for larger frames.

The duplex fitting can also house a spider converter or fitting which allows the shade to be used for both a lamp base and a pendant. This is particularly useful for large, straight-sided drum shades. It allows for the drum to be used as a standard lamp or, for example, a large feature pendant light.

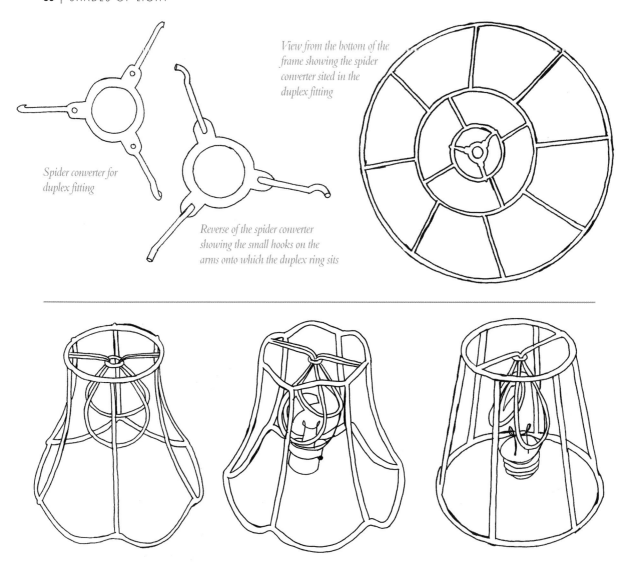

View from the bottom of the frame showing the spider converter sited in the duplex fitting

Spider converter for duplex fitting

Reverse of the spider converter showing the small hooks on the arms onto which the duplex ring sits

Above *Golf ball clip*

Above centre *The fitting clips over the golf ball bulb holding the frame in place*

Above right *Frame with candle clip fitting, clipped onto a candle bulb*

CLIPS

Whereas the duplex fitting is used on larger frames, the fittings illustrated, the candle clip and golf ball clip, are generally found on smaller, often wall sconce or chandelier, shades.

The clip simply fits over the bulb, so care must be taken to ensure that the shade doesn't tip and the bulb touch the fabric of the shade. You will often see scorch marks on the sides of these small shades where this has happened. The introduction of long-life bulbs which are often larger and a different shape than the traditional bulb has meant that sometimes these clips can't accommodate the bulb – although some long-life bulbs are becoming available in a more traditional shape.

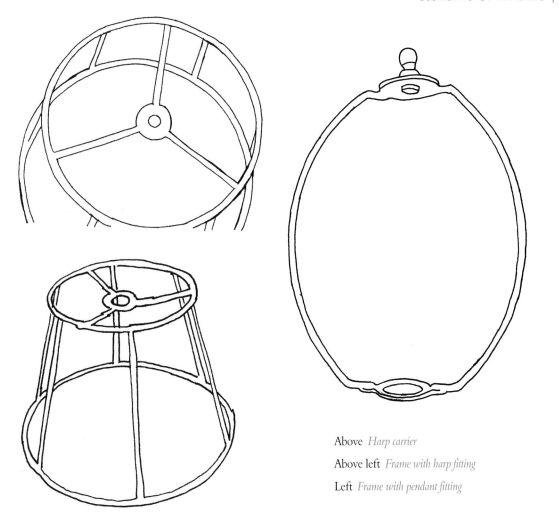

Above *Harp carrier*

Above left *Frame with harp fitting*

Left *Frame with pendant fitting*

HARP

Many American lamps have a harp fitting. This is a small aperture on top of the frame and has to be used with a harp carrier and again these are available in different heights.

The harp usually has a decorative finial which screws into the top of the harp, fixing it to the lamp and providing stability. These are usually ornamental and are made in metal, ceramic, crystal stone or wood.

A riser – a small metal disc that is available in different depths – can be screwed onto the top of the harp and raises the shade very slightly.

PENDANT FITTING

This fitting allows shades to be hung from the ceiling, or used for a lamp with an angled arm. It is attached to the top ring of the shade, sometimes slightly dropped into the body of the shade by an angled gimbal.

CHAPTER FOUR

Frame Shapes

T here is a huge variety of frame shapes, different shapes lending themselves to different techniques, so it's important to take this into consideration when making a shade. The following are the basic frame shapes which, if you alter their proportions, become your own design. As long as the frame allows a bulb to have a safe distance from the fabric (and this can vary depending on the shape and wattage of the bulb), then experiment with frame shapes. Take inspiration from your area of interest, whether that be fashion, flowers, nature etc., and be creative to produce your own unique frame shape.

Straight empire

This is a very traditional frame shape. The top ring is smaller than the bottom ring and the rings are joined by straight struts.

Straight empire

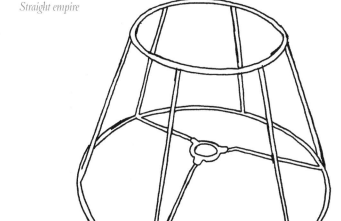

Linen straight empire with self-corsage

Scott Lewis Photography

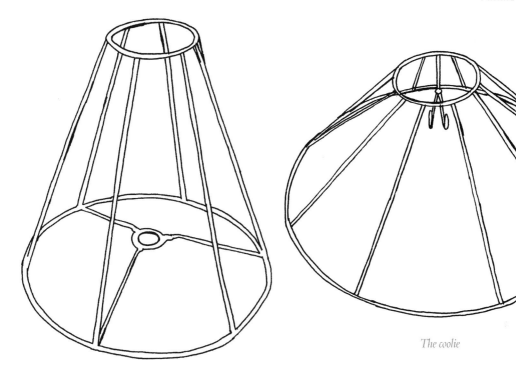

The cone or dunce

The coolie

Variations on this basic shape can be achieved by altering the proportions of the top and bottom rings and the strut length. One alteration gives rise to the cone or dunce, in which the top ring is again smaller than the bottom ring, but is joined by longer struts.

Another variation is the coolie where the top ring is significantly smaller than the bottom ring and is joined by shorter struts.

Yet another alternative is the canister drum. Here, the top ring is slightly smaller than the bottom ring and is joined by medium length struts.

Although all of these frames look different, they are essentially all straight empire frames.

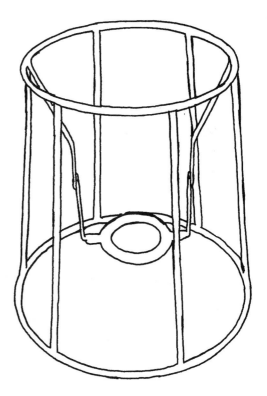

The canister drum

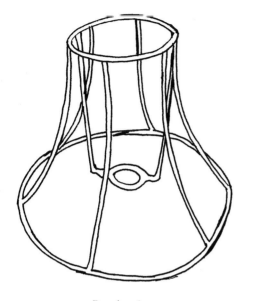

Bowed empire

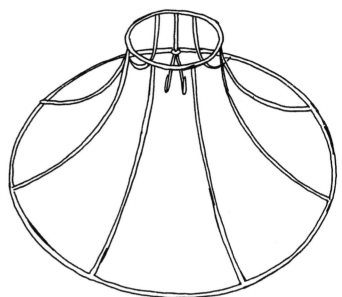

Shallow bowed empire

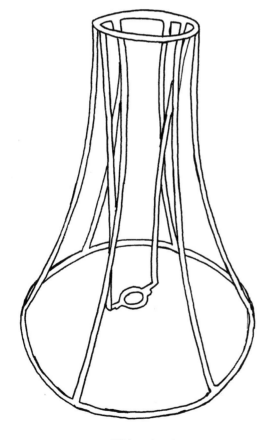

Tall bowed empire

Bowed empire

This frame shape, like the straight empire, has a top ring smaller than the bottom ring, but the struts that join the two are bowed or curved to a greater or lesser degree. As before, by adjusting the proportions of the rings and struts, different shapes can be achieved.

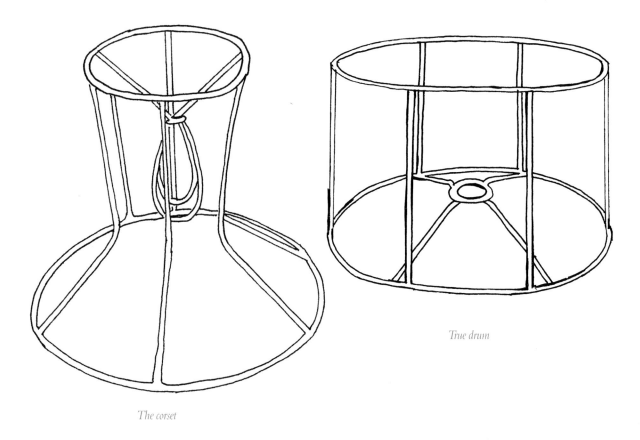

True drum

The corset

Corset

The corset shade is achieved by giving the frame a 'waist'. That is, the diameter of the waist section is smaller than that of the top ring.

Drum

A drum frame, as its name suggests, is one in which the diameter of the top ring is exactly the same as the diameter of the bottom ring. If the rings are joined by a straight strut, then this is a modern drum. This is a difficult shape for two reasons. First, frame manufacturers are reluctant to stock these frames as they don't stack: they literally have to stand one on top of the other, thus requiring a huge amount of storage space. Secondly, a true drum (where the top and bottom rings are the same diameter) gives an optical illusion when covered, that the top ring is slightly larger than the bottom ring. To adjust for this illusion and to enable them to be stacked, manufacturers often make them with the top ring very slightly smaller in diameter than the bottom ring.

By altering the proportions the drum

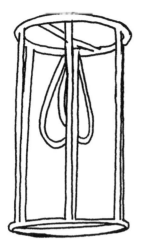

Wall sconce cylinder

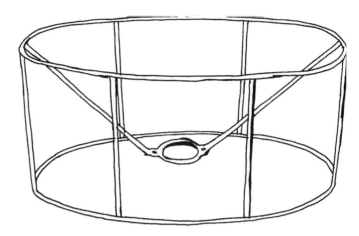

Oval shallow drum

Oval shallow drum – shallow straight-sided oval drum in a large botanical print

Scott Lewis Photography

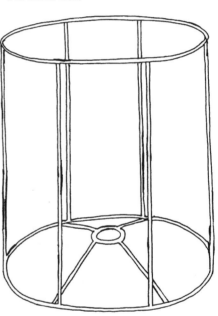

Tall oversize drum

shade can achieve lots of different looks, as shown in the accompanying illustrations.

Another variation of the drum is the bowed drum, which is effective in all sizes from small wall sconce shades to large standard lamps.

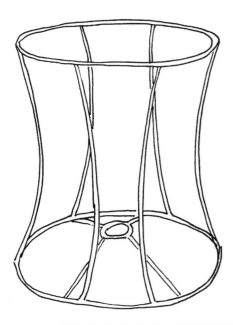

*Bowed drum. The side struts are
bowed to give a different look
from the straight-sided drum*

*Pair of bowed drums
in ruched silk dupion*

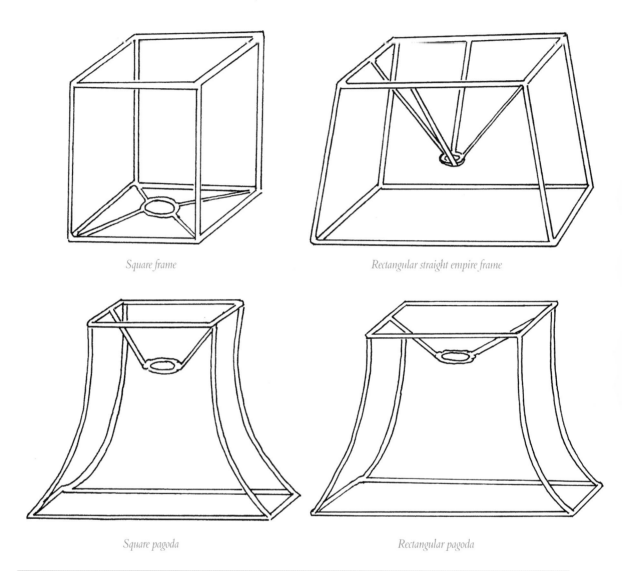

Square frame

Rectangular straight empire frame

Square pagoda

Rectangular pagoda

Square frame

As its name suggests, this is simply a frame in which the top and bottom rings are square, joined by a straight strut.

By lengthening two opposite sides of the bottom ring this gives a rectangular straight empire.

The rectangular and square frames give a modern look, whereas if you introduce a bowed strut, this gives a more traditional look, sometimes called a pagoda.

Tiffany frame   *Bell frame*

Tiffany and bell frame

Whereas all the frames so far mentioned have used a concave outer curve, the Tiffany shades use a convex outer curve.

The Tiffany shade is widely used and was particularly popular in the 1970s. It can't incorporate a balloon lining, which might account for the fact that, when used as a pendant shade, this pattern is often trimmed with very long chainette fringing on the bottom ring, making it very difficult to see up inside the unlined shade.

The bell or tulip frame is so called because of its bell- or flower-like appearance. Although it also has a convex curve it differs slightly from the Tiffany by having a slight outward curve on the bottom ring.

Tiffany shade with gallery in duchesse silk satin

Reec's School Photography Club

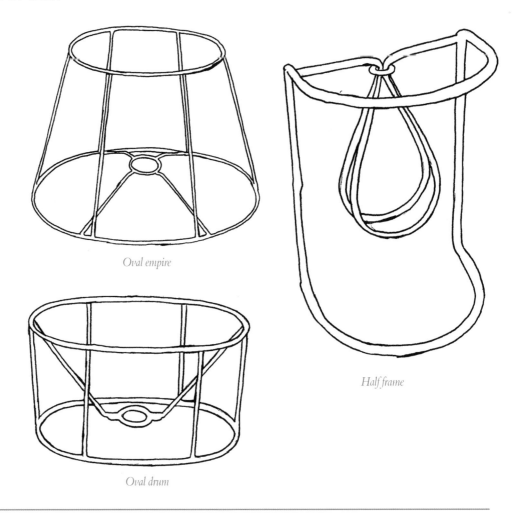

Oval empire

Half frame

Oval drum

Oval frames

An oval shape is a particularly useful frame shape, simply because it gives a pleasing curve without taking up too much space on the table on which it is placed. It is rare to be able to walk all around a shade; most shades are on a table or surface against a wall. This feature enables the oval shade to have a definite back and front and it can sit back nicely against the wall, saving space.

Rectangular frames work on the same principle and ovals and rectangles can be used within a large variety of frame shapes.

Other shapes

HALF FRAMES

The half frame or shield is a frame that is used on a wall light fixture or lamp that is sited against a wall. It simply shields the bulb from one side.

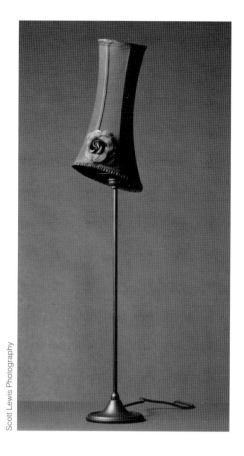

Tall black bowed empire shade with an asymmetric bottom ring

Tall bowed empire frame with asymmetric top ring

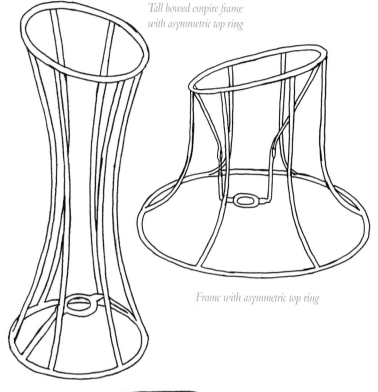

Frame with asymmetric top ring

HEXAGONAL FRAMES

These frames have a top and bottom ring of a hexagonal shape rather than a circle. This gives the effect of flat panels running from top to bottom around the shade.

ASYMMETRICAL FRAMES

All of the frames discussed so far have been symmetrical. However, if you have a willing frame-maker, then your frame designs can be more adventurous. As long as the frame will make a shade that is safe and functional, asymmetrical frames can be used to make traditionally made shades.

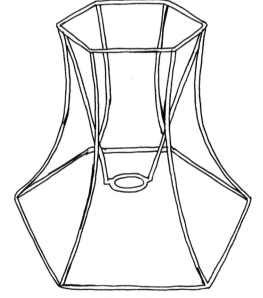

Hexagonal frame

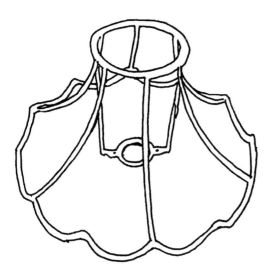

Bowed empire frame with double scallop or floral bottom ring

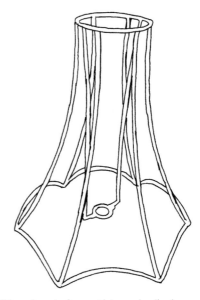

Tall bowed empire frame with inverted scallop bottom ring

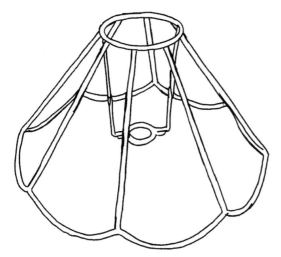

Straight empire frame with scallop bottom ring

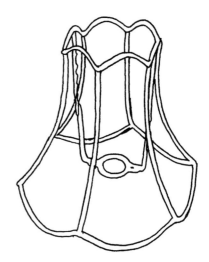

Bowed empire frame with scallop top and bottom ring

Ring variations

All of the shapes discussed so far have had plain rings; however, many frames can benefit from decorative edges, as can be seen in the accompanying illustrations.

Shades with a double ring around the bottom ring are referred to as banded or galleried frames, whereas frames with the double ring around the top ring are called collared shades. If the collar has a bottom ring of a slightly smaller diameter than its top ring, this is known as a French shade.

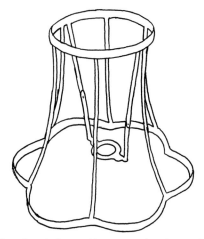

Bowed empire frame with regency or clover bottom ring

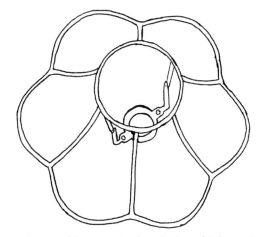

An aerial view of the regency ring shows the shape of the bottom ring

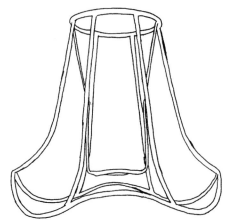

Oriental frame, showing a wave-like curve on the bottom ring

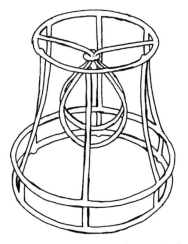

Small bowed empire sconce frame with gallery

Detail of cerise silk shade showing gallery or band

Reed's School Photography Club

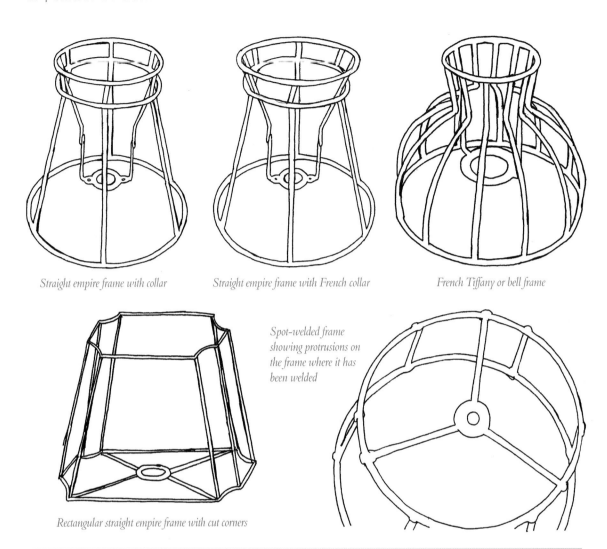

Straight empire frame with collar

Straight empire frame with French collar

French Tiffany or bell frame

Spot-welded frame showing protrusions on the frame where it has been welded

Rectangular straight empire frame with cut corners

Inverted panels on the corners of square shades are known as cut corners.

Making up frames

If you base your frame design on one of these fundamental shapes, an experienced frame-maker will be able to make up your own unique designs.

When having a frame made, the ideal way is to have the joins (where the struts meet the rings for example) braised rather than spot-welded. Although more time-consuming and therefore more expensive, the braising technique does give a better finish to a completed shade as there are fewer lumps to contend with, giving a cleaner look.

CHAPTER FIVE

Materials and Equipment Required for Shade Making

Tape, threads and ribbon

STRAIGHT FRAME TAPE

In order to pin and ultimately sew fabric onto the frame, the frame needs something to sew into. Traditionally the frame is bound with a cotton tape called straight frame tape; this is a cotton loose-weave tape. It is available in a bleached or unbleached form and in different widths: 10mm or 7mm. The thinner of the two widths (7mm) is ideal when binding smaller wall sconce shades which are made with wire of a smaller diameter.

Because it is cotton, this tape can be dyed using cold water dyes, although allow for shrinkage. This is used when making a Tiffany shade where the tape is visible. The tape can be dyed to match the outer fabric to give a good finish.

CREAM THREAD

If the lining is cream or ivory then a matching thread will be needed for sewing the lining. A polyester sew-all thread is ideal as it is slightly elastic.

COLOURED THREAD

This is thread that matches the outer fabric, again try to use a synthetic sew-all thread. Sew-all thread is generally stronger, smoother and available in a broader colour range than mercerized cotton, nylon, silk or bobbin threads.

CREAM SATIN RIBBON

Double satin cream ribbon of approx 15mm width is used to cover the raw edge on the gimbals. Approximately 10cm is needed per gimbal.

Pins, needles and thimbles

DRESSMAKING PINS

A few dressmaking pins are needed to hold layers of fabric together and to pin tracing paper onto lining fabric.

LILLS

Lills are small craft pins, sometimes known as sequin pins, and are generally 0.65mm diameter x 20 or 13mm length and are available in brass (which is rustless) or nickel-plated steel. These tiny pins are used to stretch and hold the fabric and lining onto the frame, and lampshade making involves using hundreds of these. They are fiddly and sometimes painful to use initially, but it is worth persevering as using longer pins will eventually cause lots of problems as you approach more challenging shade shapes or very small shades.

If lills really are too difficult to use then lace pins (0.53 x 26mm) or appliqué pins (0.65 x 22mm) can be used. Appliqué pins have the advantage of having a small plastic bead head which makes working with them slightly easier and although they are slightly longer than lills, they are still quite fine and a good compromise.

HAND-SEWING NEEDLES

Your choice of a straight needle is a very personal one. Experiment and find a type that suits you. For making shades the needle has to pierce many layers of fabric, so a finer longer needle is ideal – although sometimes these have a tendency to snap.

You will also need a fine curved needle for attaching any bias onto the shade. A fine curved beading needle is ideal when working with silk, and a slightly thicker one (although not as thick as a curved upholstery needle) is ideal for more substantial fabrics.

THIMBLES

Because of the amount of pinning and sewing through many layers, you may find that you initially need a thimble to protect your fingers. The traditional metal thimble has its place, but in order to maintain some of the 'feel' of the fabric and processes involved, some craftspeople prefer a leather thimble, which is much more flexible. These are available for full fingers or the tips of fingers and can also be used in conjunction with a traditional metal thimble if you place the metal thimble inside the leather one. A quilter's 'tip', which is a small metal disc, rather like the end of a traditional metal thimble, is self-adhesive and attaches to the tip of your finger and this can also protect the ends of your fingers.

Cutting tools

You will need small and large dressmaking scissors and they need to be very sharp. You may also need a pair of pinking shears for making trims. These have a zigzag saw tooth rather than a straight blade.

A rotary cutter will be needed for making bias trim. One with a 45mm diameter blade is ideal. A self-healing cutting mat is also needed if using a rotary cutter – buy the biggest that you can afford.

Trim or bias-making tool

Any trim that is used on a lampshade usually has to negotiate lots of curves and sometimes corners. Ribbons, gimp trims and braids made for curtains and soft furnishings are often unsuitable as they are made on the straight of the grain. Lampshade making usually requires a trim made on the bias. Bias binding is available to buy ready-made, but is rarely an ideal colour, fabric or width for a handmade shade, so a bias-making tool is used in lampshade making to make a self-bias trim (i.e. one made out of the same fabric as the main body of the shade) to trim the top and bottom rings.

These little tools are available in different sizes to make different band widths. You will find them in most good haberdashers, craft stores and specialist quilting shops. Electric bias-making machines are also available for longer lengths of trim.

Measuring and marking

MEASURES
A soft tape measure is needed for working out the circumference of the lampshade rings when making a trim, and a quilter's rule or grid and set square are useful when cutting a bias trim.

CALCULATOR
A calculator is a useful tool, particularly when calculating the amount of trim required on a shade. If the shade is circular the circumference of the ring can be calculated by multiplying the diameter of the ring by 3.142 (π). This saves you having to reach to measure round very large shades with a tape measure as this can be awkward and inaccurate.

MARKERS
A soft lead pencil (2B or 4B) is needed for marking fabric; it is also useful to have a white pencil when marking darker fabrics. A tailor's chalk line can be too inaccurate for lampshade making and doesn't work on the lining fabric.

SELF-ADHESIVE COLOURED STICKERS/DOTS
If you are using a plain fabric like dupion, and when making the lining, these dots are used to identify one side of the fabric from the other in order that both sides of the shade are made using the same side of the fabric. Small self-adhesive sheets of dots are available from stationers.

Machines

IRON
A steam iron is preferable; make sure the plate is clean and free from any snags which could damage fine fabrics.

SEWING MACHINE

With both the tailored and kitchen shades a straight machine stitch is all that is required, so a basic sewing machine is perfectly adequate.

Tracing paper

Strips of tracing paper 4cm wide are very useful in lampshade making as these save you from having to keep changing the needle on your sewing machine when sewing jersey linings. Ordinarily, when sewing fabric the point of the needle pierces the threads in the fabric to go through to the other side. When sewing jersey fabrics, because of the huge amount of give or stretch in the threads, the point of the needle bounces off the surface of the thread and doesn't go through to the other side to catch the bobbin thread coming from the underside of the machine. This results in missed stitches and subsequent gaps in the seam of the lining. In order to get round this you can change the needle to a jersey needle or ballpoint needle, which has a rounded tip that penetrates the fabric by forcing apart the warp and weft threads without catching or cutting the threads. Alternatively you can use a stretch needle and a running foot on your machine, which is good for sewing through tightly knitted jersey fabrics or those with a high elastine content (trade names Lycra and Spandex). These stretch needles create a longer thread loop before forming the stitch, thereby decreasing the chance of a missed stitch. Some machines will have a stretch stitch facility but if yours doesn't then a very narrow zigzag stitch will suffice. The zigzag allows your fabric to stretch but it is important to test it on some of your jersey lining fabric to find out which is the best result.

However, if you sew your jersey lining with a straight stitch through a piece of tracing paper with a normal sewing machine needle, this appears to solve the problem. This has the advantage of still being able to use a straight stitch; it allows you to draw a sewing line on the tracing paper, to guide you to make the lining seams more symmetrical and prevents you from having to change the needle frequently.

Glue

Very little glue is used in traditional lampshade making. A basic glue stick (paper glue) can be used to seal stitches during one stage of the process and a quick, clear-drying strong glue is sometimes needed if a bought trim is used to trim the rings – this glue is used to butt the two ends of the trim together to form a seal and stop the trim from fraying. A gel glue is ideal for this as it doesn't 'string', but these are harder to obtain. If you prefer, you need not use any glue at all.

Other equipment and sourcing

Other non-essential equipment that you might find useful could include a needle threader, a magnetic pin cushion and tweezers. Most of the equipment needed is found in the home, in a basic household sewing kit, or is readily available in high street retailers. The only specialist items you may need to purchase are lills, a bias-making tool, curved needles, rotary cutter and self-healing cutting mat.

CHAPTER SIX

Fabric

The choice of fabric for lampshade making is very important. Fabrics need to be flexible enough to be able to negotiate curves and stretch around a frame and be substantial enough to withstand the stretching and last in place for about twenty-five years. Choosing fabric that is suitable for lampshade making is so important because if you choose something unsuitable, it is going to make your first attempts problematical and you may become unnecessarily disappointed and disillusioned.

There are various things to consider and these include the weight of the fabric, the weave and subsequent texture, the width, the pattern (and any embellishment), whether it is colour-fast and, of course, price. All of these considerations will be explored in order that you make a good choice for your project.

The first important factor is to choose a woven or knitted fabric rather than a felted or bonded one. Weaving or knitting threads creates the pliable material that is fabric. Woven fabric is produced by interlacing yarns, and knitted fabrics are produced by interlooping yarns. But fabrics can also be made by felting, whereby wool fibres, fur, and synthetic materials are pressed together with heat, moisture and agitation and this produces a condensed, matted, felted

material. This is not particularly pliable, strong or even in texture so is not a good choice for shade making, although it makes for very effective embellishments as it has structure, texture and doesn't fray.

Pattern and bias

Most lampshades made in the traditional way require the fabric to 'hug' the frame when stretching tightly over it. In order to get this stretch, fabrics are generally used on the cross or 'bias'. This is where the fabric is used at a 45-degree angle to the warp and weft threads. Woven fabric has two sets of threads running perpendicular to one another. The ones that run from the top to the bottom of the fabric are called the warp threads and the ones that run from left to right (from selvedge to selvedge) are called the weft threads. If you pull in either of these directions the fabric is usually fairly inflexible and strong. However, if you pull at a 45-degree angle across these threads, then the fabric has much greater stretch and elasticity and it is this 'bias' or 'cross' line that is used when making a lampshade. It maintains the strength of the fabric whilst allowing the elasticity needed for negotiating around the curves of a frame.

Using fabric on the bias does, however, cause problems in that a fabric with a definite pattern running along the straight of grain will not be able to be kept straight on the shade, as it has to be used at a 45-degree angle.

In this situation it is best to choose a frame shape in which there are few curves to negotiate and the fabric can be used on the straight of the grain, thereby keeping the pattern straight. This is also why striped fabrics are difficult to use unless they're used on a straight-sided drum. Plain fabrics, florals and those with a more random design that doesn't run in a particular direction are ideal. It is worth noting here that there are two side seams on a tailored lampshade and because the fabric is used on the cross, it is not possible to pattern-match these seams as it is with curtain making. This is not

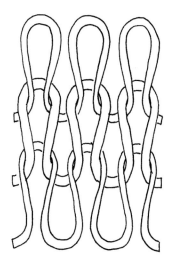

Knitted structure

These diagrams show the differences between the structure of knitted and woven fabrics

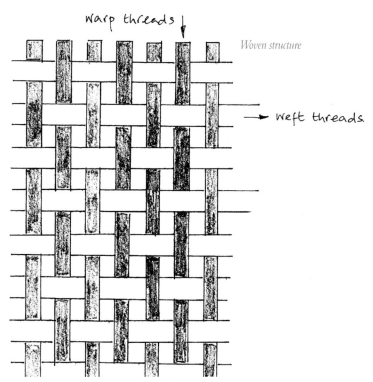

Woven structure

usually a problem, however, as lampshades are not positioned on their lamp base with the side seam foremost; they should be positioned with the side seams to the side.

There is quite a lot of wastage of fabric when shades are made on the bias, so this is worth considering if the fabric is very expensive.

Weight, texture and embellishment

Fabrics that split or tear easily are not suitable for shade making. The fabric is under a lot of tension whilst stretched over a frame so it needs to be robust. Vintage fabrics are particularly prone to tearing as the fibres disintegrate over time. A tailored silk lampshade made with new silk should last about twenty-five years before the silk starts to break down. If you do want to use a vintage fabric, hold it up to the light (natural is best) and this will enable you to detect stains, moth holes and thin, worn sections of fabric that wouldn't be robust enough but might not be apparent until the shade was completed and lit.

Fabrics that have too loose a weave are often unsuccessful in shade making, for example, loose weave linens, hopsack-type fabrics, laces and devorés. This is partly because it is possible to see a lot of the bulb when it is lit through the gaps in the weave. By their very nature, these types of fabrics have lots of extra 'give' and are hard to stretch completely evenly, and this shows as a wavy line along the grain rather than a straight one. As with a lot

of these examples, problems only become apparent when the shade is lit. An unlit shade is much more forgiving, but rather loses its purpose.

Jacquard fabric, in which the design is an integral part of the weave of the fabric, is very successful when lit. The design is highlighted when back lit and gives a completely different look from when it is unlit.

Fabrics with a nap or pile, such as velvets and furs, are often very dense and therefore difficult to manipulate. This also applies to tweeds and heavy twills. They allow very little light through them, so the light tends to be thrown above and below the shade. Also the two side seams on the shade are under great tension and tend to part the nap or pile at this point, which is not ideal.

Heavily embroidered fabrics are also awkward to use as it's very difficult to obtain a completely smooth finish. The fabric will tend to stretch at a particular rate where there isn't any embroidery, but stretch less where the embroidery section is, as the embroidery threads are holding the fabric fast. Puckers are often the result and a uniformly taut shade is difficult to achieve.

Fabrics that have been fireproofed tend to be very inflexible as a result of the fireproofing process (in which the fabric is impregnated with fire-retardant chemicals), so although they would appear a safe choice they are not prac-tical. Fabrics can, however, be fire-retarded with a spray chemical once they are finished and the fabric has been stretched. These sprays are available in hardware shops and haberdasheries.

Colour-fastness

If your shade is likely to be in an environment where it is going to get dirty, dusty or yellowed by cigarette smoke, it might be worth choosing a washable fabric. Handmade tailored lampshades can be washed with care (see Chapter 26 for more on laundering). To minimize any risk of bleeding it is important to check first whether the fabric is colour-fast.

Colour

Lampshades are meant to be illuminated so it is useful, when deciding on a fabric for a shade, to shine a light source through it. Consider taking a torch with you when shopping for fabric to give you an idea, as fabrics can look very different when lit and unlit. When illuminated, the design on some fabrics really comes to the fore, whereas others can be 'bleached out' by the light.

Different coloured fabrics give different lights. To some extent this depends on the size and shape of the shade, as this partly determines where the light is thrown, but colour is an important factor to take into consider-ation. Fabrics in the red spectrum give a warm, cosy light, whereas blues and greens give a fresher light, but some consider it 'colder' light. Green shades can sometimes give an eerie light – so test beforehand. Creams and golds are the most popular colours. They allow lots of light through the shade and the gold still gives a warm, softer light. It is possible, however, to buy cream lampshades very easily, so if you are going to go to the trouble of making one, consider being a little more adventurous!

Price and width

Lampshade making, unlike many other soft furnishing techniques such as curtain making and loose covers, does not require a lot of fabric. It is entirely possible to make a very successful medium-sized lampshade from half a metre of fabric, so fabric remnants can easily be used. Because of the small amount needed you may also consider experimenting with perhaps a section from a piece of clothing, silk scarves, table linens, shirting, ticking and other utility fabrics; always bearing in mind the constraints of these fabrics with regard to weave and vintage.

It is worth noting that although fabrics usually are sold in standard widths of 137cm, occasionally silk fabrics are sold in many other widths owing to the different looms they are produced on. Silk is available in widths such as 110cm, 114cm, 120cm, 135cm, 140cm, to 150cm and this is worth bearing in mind when planning your shade.

Traditionally lampshades are made in silk. Silk dupion is a really good fabric to use as it has an attractive slub that runs through the fabric, which gives it a bit of texture. It is available in a huge range of colours and is at the cheaper end of the price range for silks. It can have a tendency to fray badly, so extra care needs to be taken with any seams. This fabric is very forgiving for a beginner, as it is strong and has a matt effect when stretched and this can hide any slight imperfections when first starting, whereas shiny fabrics such as silk satins and taffetas show every slight wrinkle or 'bubble' as they reflect the light. The matt finish of a dupion silk also prevents it slipping when sewing onto the frame. Because of these qualities and price, it is a good starting fabric for a beginner. As you become more experienced you will become more adept at knowing whether a fabric will be suitable and, as is the case with a lot of these fabric crafts, there is really no substitute for touch and handling, so if you are buying through a wholesaler always ask for samples first.

CHAPTER SEVEN

Lining Fabric

Most traditionally made lampshades are lined. The lining usually hides the struts, rings and seams on the inside of the shade, particularly in pendant shades, and gives a smooth, clean look. It gives a depth or substance to the cover, diffuses the light so you can't see the filament of the bulb, and increases the amount of light being reflected out of the shade. If you use coloured linings, these can also change the colour of the light being reflected out; golds, pinks and reds give a warm glow. Lining can also be used decoratively, either to become apparent through the outer cover as the design on the lining shines through when the lamp is lit, or when looking up inside a pendant shade to see a patterned fabric.

There are three main types of lining method.

Balloon or internal lining

This is the main type of lining used in traditional shade making. It conceals all of the struts and seams of a shade, but it is not possible to use it on all types of frame, most notably the Tiffany-shaped frame. Very small wall sconce or chandelier shades are also sometimes unsuitable as the lining may be too close to the bulb to be safe.

External lining

This is a lining sited on the outside of the struts and can be used on Tiffany and wall sconce shades. The struts of the shade are still visible, but the seams on the outer cover are concealed.

Pleated/ruched lining

This is often used as a design feature, for example in a large pendant shade over a dining table, the interest being on the inside of the frame rather than the outside. Fabric is ruched or pleated on the inside of the shade and is primarily decorative. Dupions and chiffons are used for this type of lining, rather than jerseys.

Materials suitable for lampshade linings

A traditional balloon lining was made of silk Habotai, but in order to negotiate frames with lots of curves it is often easier to use a double-knit jersey fabric as it is so stretchy. It gives a really smooth, neat finish inside the shade. Single-knit jerseys can be prone to laddering and snagging, so a double-knit jersey is generally better as it is a very stable fabric and unlikely to ladder or run. Fine double-knit jerseys can, however, be hard to obtain. Mills that supply dancewear manufacturers and use elastine are worth seeking out if you intend to buy the fabric in bulk by the bale. Silk double-knit jersey is readily available through specialist silk suppliers and offers a variety of colours, but is very expensive.

Alternatively, if you need a small amount of lining for a single shade, or want a small amount of a particular colour, particularly peaches, pinks or black, cutting up a large under-slip or petticoat can be a good compromise. Lingerie manufacturers use a lot of double-knit jerseys because of their stretch. Other stretch fabrics which are available include viscose linens, stretch cotton and cotton satin, stretch peach skin, stretch satin, viscose jersey and cotton jersey, although their elasticity varies, so test first.

Lampshades can also be balloon-lined with light dress-weight fabrics but although the technique used is exactly the same as when using a stretchy fabric, it is much more difficult to achieve a smooth finish. The template needs to be very accurate. It is, however, becoming much more popular to have a plain outer cover and patterned lining, particularly with pendant shades or clusters of pendant shades where the detail becomes apparent when you look up inside them.

CHAPTER EIGHT

Binding

Lampshade frames are bound with cotton straight frame tape to provide a surface on the metal into which you can pin and ultimately sew fabric onto the frame. The binding forms the very basis of the lampshade so it needs to be smooth, tight, even and secure. Loose binding will allow the fabric to slip and gives a loose cover. Because the binding is the first process in making a shade, this is a very difficult problem to rectify, so it is worth spending time on the binding to get it right and tight!

First, make sure the frame is sound, clean and symmetrical. If you have a plastic-coated or painted frame you need only bind the top and bottom rings and two opposite side struts. (These side strut bindings are usually temporary and are removed when the shade is being assembled.) If, however, you are using an uncoated frame, you will need to bind all of the struts and rings and these remain in place for the life of the shade.

If you are binding an uncoated frame, you will need to bind all of the struts first and then the top and bottom rings. This gives a cleaner finish to the rings as the loose ends of the strut knots can be covered up by the top and bottom ring bindings. You don't need to bind the fitting or the gimbals, although it can make for a more uniform look.

Method

Measure the circumference of the ring you are to bind and cut 2½–3 times this amount of tape. If, for example, a ring has a circumference of 60cm you will need approximately 150–180cm of tape. Each person's binding varies slightly, so eventually you will be able to gauge whether you require more or less tape. The amount of tape also depends on the gauge of wire used in making the lampshade. The smaller wall sconce frames are made from much thinner wire than larger frames, so they don't need quite so much tape. Larger standard shades are made from a much more robust wire, which has a larger diameter, and some frames have a flat metal band on the top and bottom rings instead of a wire; these are usually manufactured shades in

Binding a frame with a flat band. This requires more tape because of the width of the band

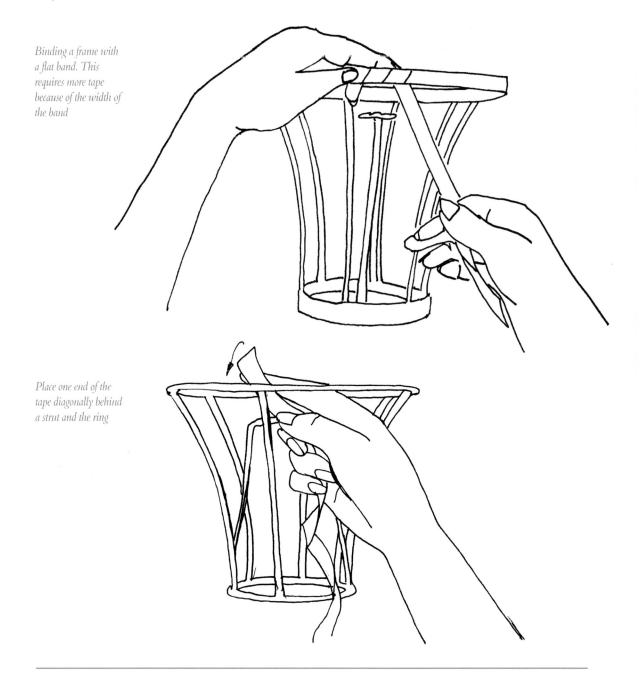

Place one end of the tape diagonally behind a strut and the ring

which the original fabric has been glued onto the frame. These flat sections require more tape; at least three times the circumference of the ring.

Bind the top and bottom rings with straight frame tape. It doesn't matter which ring you bind first. Make a knot on the ring which also incorporates one of the struts; this anchors the knot so it

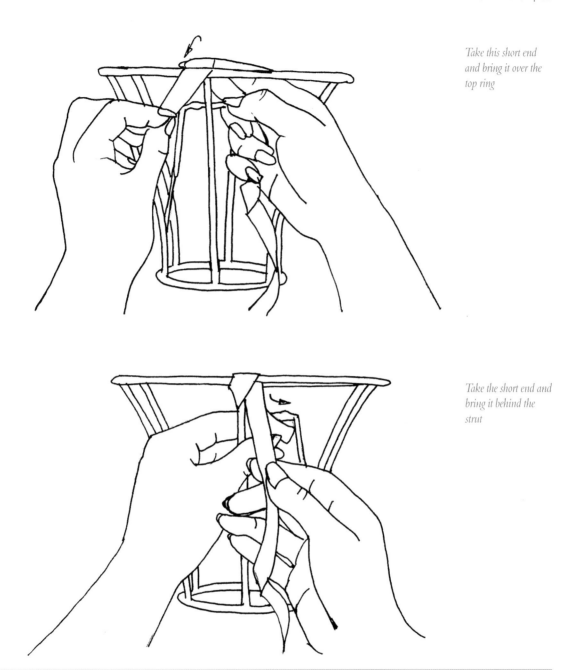

Take this short end and bring it over the top ring

Take the short end and bring it behind the strut

doesn't slide around the ring. Avoid making the knot by one of the gimbals as this can cause extra bulk. Cut the short end of the tape to about 2cm and, when tying the knot, always move this short end to create the knot, keeping the long end still. This knot needs to be secure and flat.

Then wrap the long piece of tape over the ring, overlapping about a third

*Bring the short end
round to the front and
put it through the loop
created by the longer
section*

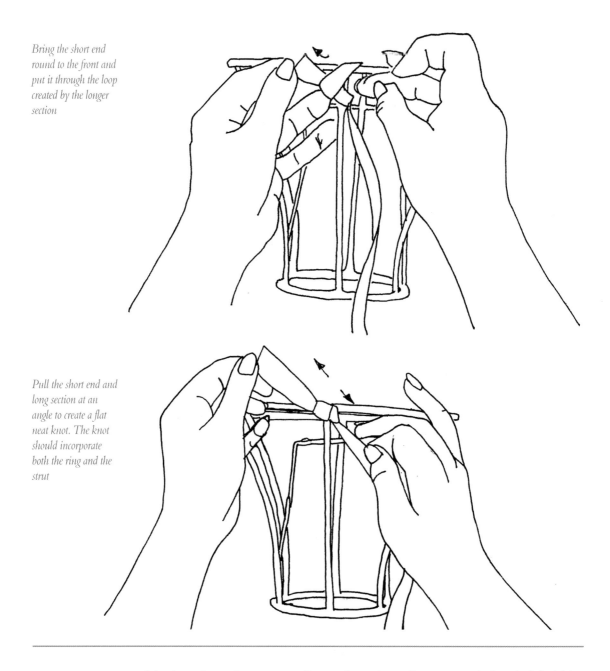

*Pull the short end and
long section at an
angle to create a flat
neat knot. The knot
should incorporate
both the ring and the
strut*

of the last piece of tape on a diagonal slant. Try to maintain the same angle of slant throughout. Don't overlap too much otherwise the binding will become too thick and bulky. Pull the tape as tightly as possible as you go along. If you are right-handed, hold the last loop of the tape down tightly with the thumb and forefinger of your left hand, whilst your right hand loops the tape over. It is much easier to wrap tape over rather than under.

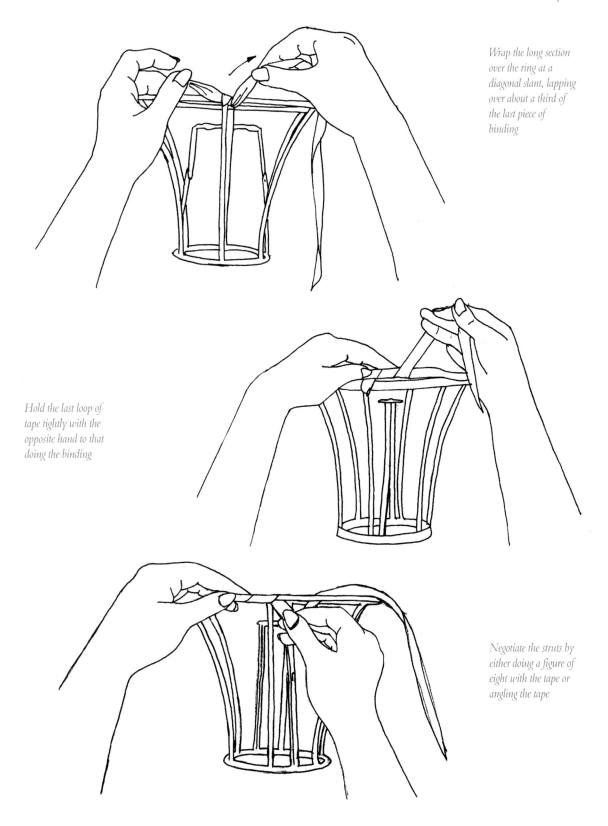

Wrap the long section over the ring at a diagonal slant, lapping over about a third of the last piece of binding

Hold the last loop of tape tightly with the opposite hand to that doing the binding

Negotiate the struts by either doing a figure of eight with the tape or angling the tape

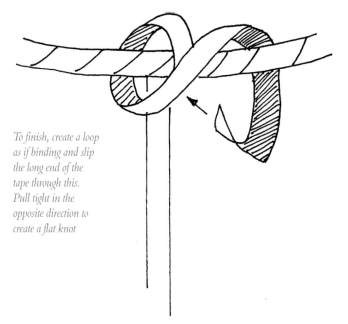

To finish, create a loop as if binding and slip the long end of the tape through this. Pull tight in the opposite direction to create a flat knot

Continue around the ring, negotiating the struts as best you can, either by doing a figure of eight around the strut or angling the tape to cover the area where the strut meets the ring. The main aim is not to have any gaps in the binding. To make sure the binding is tight enough, take a bound section between your thumb and forefinger and try to twist it in both directions. If it moves, then it is probably worth doing the binding again.

As you near the end of the ring, incorporate the short end of the first knot (cut to 2cm) by binding over it and then finish by tying a flat knot, the same as for the beginning, over the original knot.

Pull the long end of the tape back on itself to flatten further. Secure this

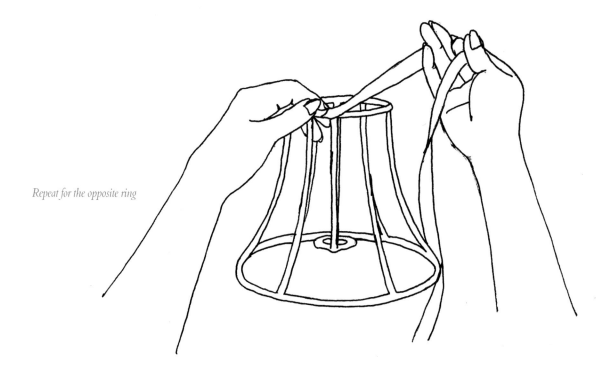

Repeat for the opposite ring

double-layered knot with a few over-stitches in cream thread and then cut the tape close to neaten.

Repeat on the opposite ring.

When binding the two opposite side struts, bear in mind that these are where the side seam will be sited, so choose the two struts that are nearest the gimbals. A shade is usually placed on a lamp with the gimbals at the side and not facing forward.

Bind these two side struts in the same way, but as these are temporary there is no need to sew the knots to secure; this just makes them more difficult to undo. You can also leave a longer piece of tape after knotting; there is no need to cut it close. Again, this eases the undoing of the knots.

The frame should now have both top and bottom rings bound and secured with a couple of stitches (these stay on for the life of the shade) and two opposite side struts bound with the ends of the tape left long for ease of undoing. (These are temporary and will be removed.)

Notes

It is sometimes an idea to angle the frame whilst binding, perhaps on your lap or between your knees, particularly when binding the side struts. Crafts-people tend to find their own comfortable position, whether it be standing or having the frame on a table, but if you are struggling to get the angle of the binding, then perhaps angle the frame.

If you calculate the amount of binding incorrectly and you run out, there are two options; either knot the binding at the nearest strut, cut a new piece of binding and start where you finished off, or keep the binding tight (ask someone to hold it for you, pin or peg it) and sew another piece onto it and continue. Both options work well.

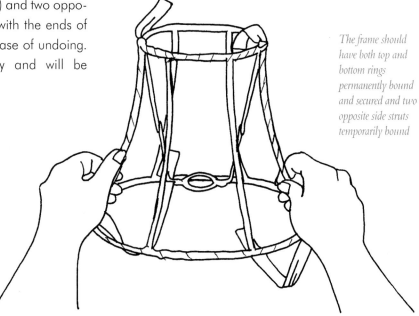

The frame should have both top and bottom rings permanently bound and secured and two opposite side struts temporarily bound

CHAPTER NINE

Making a Balloon Lining

A balloon lining and the outer cover are made in the same way, although when learning it is advisable to make the lining first in order to learn the technique, as jersey is a much more forgiving fabric than that used for the top cover. Jersey has a knitted construction and as a result of this is very stretchy, so it doesn't need to be used on the bias or cross. Also, as it can be used on the straight of the grain, it is much more economical.

The lining (as with the main cover) is made in two halves. Many jerseys look the same on both sides but, just like woven fabrics, have a face and a back, two different sides, one being slightly shinier than the other. This often only becomes apparent when sited in the shade, by which time it is too late to change it. It is therefore an idea to identify which side of the lining fabric you'd like to use at the outset. You can do this by using small stickers, perhaps self-adhesive dots, to identify which side is which.

To give a rough estimate of the amount of lining you will need, measure the depth of the frame using a soft tape measure to hug into the curves and add 10cm. Then measure half of the circumference of the bottom ring and add 12cm.

Cut out the fabric to these measurements and then drape it over half the shade, 'wrong' side out, from bound side strut to opposite bound strut, covering the top and bottom rings in the process.

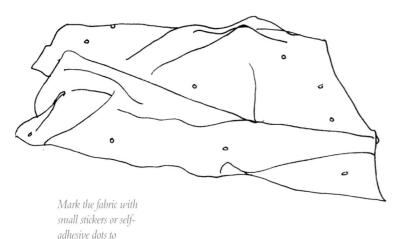

Mark the fabric with small stickers or self-adhesive dots to identify which side of the lining to use

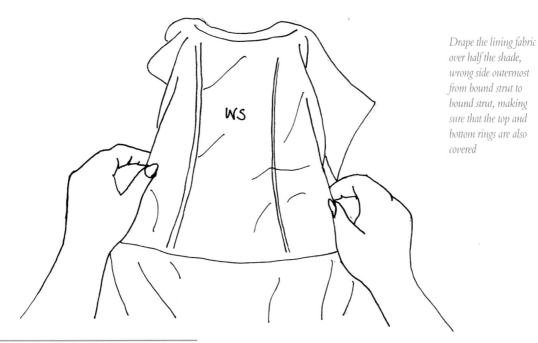

Drape the lining fabric over half the shade, wrong side outermost from bound strut to bound strut, making sure that the top and bottom rings are also covered

With the lills, pin the lining onto the four 'corners' of the shade. The lills need to go through the lining fabric and into the binding tape and out again. The lills mustn't go through to the back of the frame. You have then sited the lining onto the frame and can begin making it taut.

Gradually pin the lining fabric onto the frame, stretching evenly as you go. Try to avoid pinning all down one side and then the other; it is best to spread the pins all around the area being stretched and gently stretch it out evenly. This gives a much more even stretch all over and prevents one area being pulled too tight. Although the lining is easy to stretch to a smooth finish, its downside is that it will just keep on giving and may become over-stretched. Fabrics containing elastine

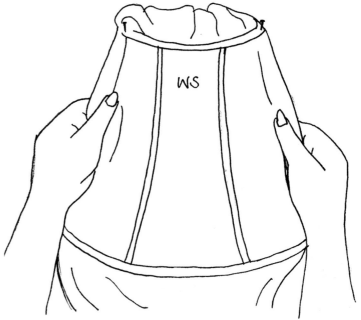

Firstly site the lining onto half the frame with four lills, one in each 'corner' where the two bound side struts meet the top and bottom rings

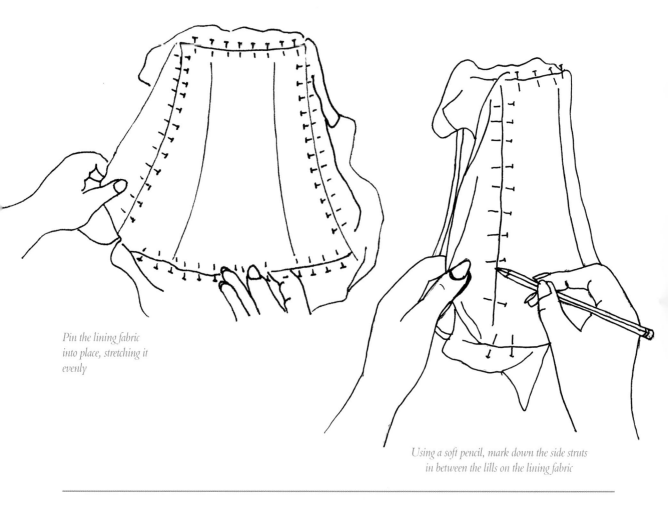

Pin the lining fabric into place, stretching it evenly

Using a soft pencil, mark down the side struts in between the lills on the lining fabric

can be stretched anywhere between four and seven times their length before they start to become overstretched, but the possibility is worth bearing in mind. You should end up with a pin every centimetre on both side struts and top and bottom rings.

Once you have a fairly taut, smooth, evenly stretched lining, with a bit of 'give' (the feeling, I've been told by a student, is rather like testing whether a sponge cake is ready or not; a small amount of 'give' that gently bounces back!), take a soft pencil (2B or 4B) and mark a broken line between the pins down the two side struts.

There is no need to mark the top and bottom rings; just put a small dot where the strut meets the ring on both the top and bottom rings.

Remove the pins and the section of lining. Don't be alarmed; this can look very disappointing. The marked lines tend to be very wobbly and the piece of lining looks very insignificant, but this is to be expected.

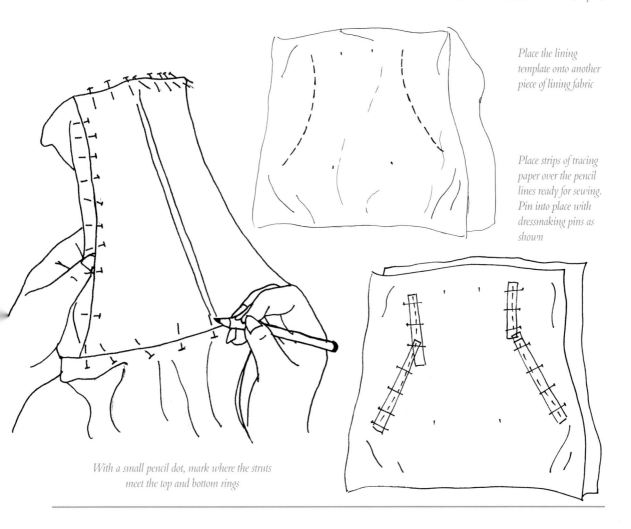

Place the lining template onto another piece of lining fabric

Place strips of tracing paper over the pencil lines ready for sewing. Pin into place with dressmaking pins as shown

With a small pencil dot, mark where the struts meet the top and bottom rings

Place this lining template 'right' side to 'right' side on another piece of lining fabric, matching the grain lines as much as possible.

Place a strip of tracing paper over the pencil lines to sew and, with dressmaking pins, pin across the tracing paper at a 90-degree angle so that the sewing machine can sew over the pins, through the tracing paper and the lining fabric.

Machine about 3mm inside the pencil lines and sew an extra 4cm at the top of the lines and 4cm at the bottom, extrapolating the lines as best you can. Although sewing through tracing paper is very effective, it is not always 100% successful so, to avoid any gaps in the seam of the lining, an extra security measure is to turn the lining fabric round once you have sewn it and go over the line again in the opposite direction.

When sewing the lining, a good tip to stop it puckering is to gently ease the fabric apart in the opposite direction

Ease the fabric apart with your hands whilst sewing on the machine to avoid puckering

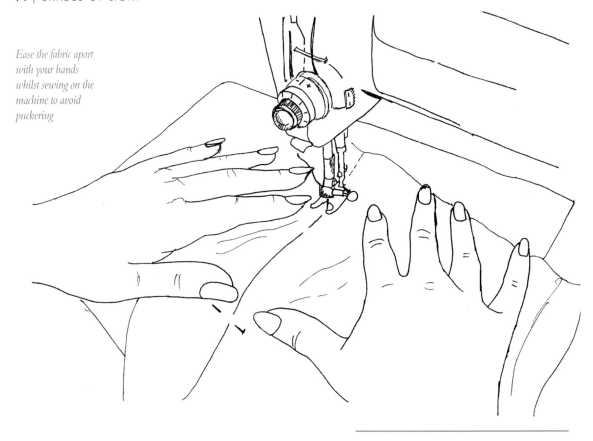

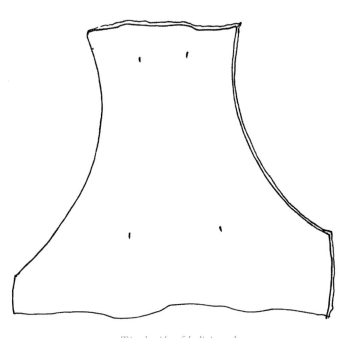

Trim the sides of the lining only

from the way in which it is being sewn. So, for example, if it is being sewn 'north to south', then gently stretch the fabric both 'west' and 'east' at the same time.

Remove the tracing paper by tearing the strips towards the stitch line and trim the lining on the sides (cutting off the pencil line if possible) very close. Do not cut anything off the top and bottom.

Remove the sticker dots. The lining is now made and needs to be put to one side. Because it looks rather insignificant it is important to put it somewhere safe as it can easily end up being thrown away with the rest of the lining scraps!

CHAPTER TEN

Making Other Types of Lining

T here are some situations in which a balloon lining either isn't possible or appropriate for the shade design. This is usually to do with shade shape – Tiffany, rectangular or square shades require a different type of lining – or where the lining is to be a decorative feature rather than purely functional.

Making a lining for a square or rectangular shade

A traditional balloon lining only has two seams and, as such, doesn't work within a square or rectangular frame as these frames need four seams in each corner to accommodate their shape. There are two ways of doing this.

METHOD 1

This is rather like making the outer cover of the sectional shade itself and, as with the traditional way of making a tailored shade, the lining must be made first. However, in this case, the lining is attached first before the outer cover is sewn on. This lining goes over the outside of the struts so they are visible, so it is a good idea to have dyed the binding tape to match the lining. Stretch each panel of lining fabric onto the outer side of the frame, pin taut and

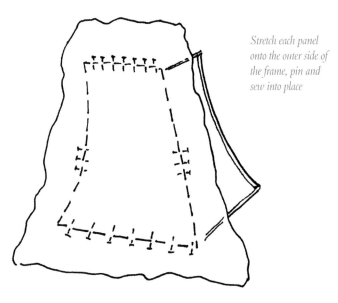

Stretch each panel onto the outer side of the frame, pin and sew into place

sew directly onto the frame. Trim close and repeat for the other panels.

METHOD 2

This method is slightly more challenging in that it needs to be very accurate in order to give a good result. It does, however, fit like a balloon lining and hides the struts.

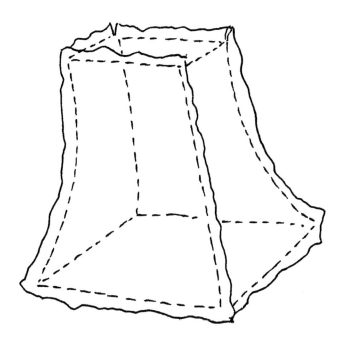

Lining with four panels for a rectangular frame

Stretch the lining fabric on a panel as before, mark with a soft pencil a broken line down each strut, remove and number each panel. Tack the linings together in the correct sequence and machine together, sewing about 3mm inside the pencil lines. The resulting lining will have four panels if the frame is square or rectangular. Trim the seams close to 3mm and then treat as a balloon lining and insert the same way, taking great care to make sure each seam lies along its corresponding strut. This is very important as a wayward lining seam will become very apparent when the shade is lit.

Gathered linings

Gathered linings are a good way of providing some interest on the inside of a shade, particularly when it is the inside of the shade that is most seen – for example in pendant shades over a feature such as a dining or snooker table. From a design point of view it is best to keep the outer cover very simple and plain if the lining is to be gathered. Detail on the outer cover, whether that be surface embellishment or pattern, would fight against any gathering on the inside, especially when lit.

There are two slightly different methods depending on whether the frame is a true drum or an empire, but with both of these shapes the external tailored cover must be made first and attached to the frame. For this type of lining it is best to use a fabric that is soft enough to ruche or pleat, but not too sheer, as the lining still has to hide the seams from the tailored cover. If you do decide to use a chiffon or georgette, the ruching must be very dense to give the coverage needed.

DRUM

If the shade is a true drum (i.e. the top ring is the same circumference as the bottom ring) measure the height of the drum and add 10cm (5cm for top handling and 5cm for the bottom handling); this is the depth of fabric to cut.

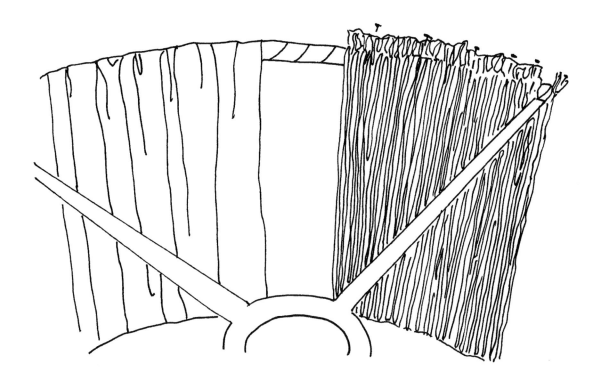

Two different lining techniques, soft relaxed fabric ruching
and fine dense chiffon ruching on the inside of a drum shade

Measure the circumference of the frame and multiply by 2½–3 times depending on the fullness of gathering required. (This can differ from fabric to fabric so it is worth experimenting with a small sample to see how the fabric gathers.) This is the length of the fabric to cut and it will probably have to be cut in strips as the fabric may not be wide enough.

With pins, divide these strips into sections that have to fit into each section of the frame. This makes sure the lining has equal amounts of fabric in each section and will make the gathering look more even.

Fold over the first strip and pin top and bottom against a strut, keeping the 5cm handling at the top and bottom. Then proceed to pin the lining into place using the pins to guide the amount in each gathered section. Keep checking, by lighting the shade, that there are no sparse or heavy areas of gathering. Sew into place on the outer side of the frame by rolling the gathered fabric over the edge of the tailored cover and trim. There will be a lot of bulk of fabric around these top and bottom rings, so any embellishment trim will need to be wide enough and substantial enough to accommodate this.

First pin the band of lining onto the bottom ring of the empire frame

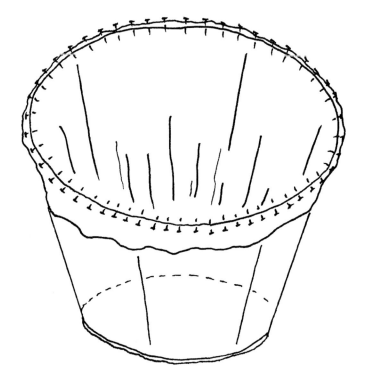

EMPIRE

Measure the height of the frame as before and add 10cm for handling. This is the depth of fabric to cut.

Measure the circumference of the larger bottom ring and add 4cm for turnings and a small contingency. This is the width of fabric to cut. Join this strip into a continuous band by machining a regular seam. Pin this band onto the bottom ring, the raw edges of the seam innermost and against a strut, and this lining should just fit round the lower ring. Sew the band into place onto the bottom ring.

Turn the frame upside down and pull the lining up inside the frame, again rolling the fabric over the top ring to pin. You will need to make small gathers or pleats on this top ring in order to accommodate all of the fabric onto the ring. Try to make the gathers or pleats as even as possible.

Sew into place again on the outer side of the frame, trim close and cover with a trim.

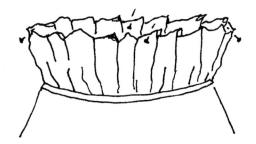

Make small gathers on the top ring to accommodate all of the fabric

Sew the lining into place on the outermost side of the ring so the stitches can be covered with a trim

External lining

This lining is used for Tiffany-shaped frames where a balloon lining can't be used. It is a lining that is sited on the outside of the frame, so the binding is visible, but it does give a seam-free look to the inside of a shade, which an unlined shade cannot do. It also provides some depth to the outer fabric so the light is better diffused. An external lining is made in exactly the same way as the outer cover, but is attached first. Instead of the seams being placed innermost when siting back on the frame as is done with the outer cover, the raw edge of the lining seam is outermost. This raw edge of this seam is hidden when the tailored cover is attached on top of it.

CHAPTER ELEVEN

Making the Outer Cover

T he outer or top cover of the shade is made in a very similar way to the lining, except that the fabric will probably have to be on the cross or bias as it will be less inclined to stretch. The cover, as with the lining, is made in two halves.

First, as before, measure the depth of the frame using a soft tape measure to hug into the curves and add 20cm. Then measure half of the circumference of the bottom ring and add 20cm.

Drape the fabric over half of the frame from bound side strut to opposite bound side strut, covering the top and bottom rings. The fabric must be on the cross

straight of grain

bias.

N\s.

This time the fabric has to be cut on the cross to give it some stretch. Cut out the fabric to these measurements and then drape over half the shade, *'wrong' side out*, from bound side strut to opposite bound strut, covering the top and bottom rings in the process. If the fabric is on the cross there will be a triangle of fabric pointing up from the top ring.

If you prefer, you need not cut the fabric at this stage, you can simply site the frame and start to pin, cutting off some of the excess later as your template starts to take shape.

As before, pin the fabric to half of the frame with the lills, starting with the four corners. Make sure that the pins are going through the fabric and catching the binding. 'Floating' lills are no use at all. Persevere until you have a smooth, taut finish. This will take much longer than before and many more pins, as the fabric is less willing to stretch. If you have a persistent 'bubble' or wrinkle in the fabric, follow the grain line from where the problem is (this is usually in a diagonal direction if the fabric is being used on the bias) and re-pin this small section at the top and bottom rings. This should make it lie flat.

With a soft pencil, mark a broken line between the pins on both side struts and put a dot where the strut meets the ring on the top and bottom rings, as was done with the lining.

Remove all the pins and place the fabric template 'right' sides together on another piece of fabric (also on the bias) matching the grain lines. This is very important as the bias is needed for the stretch and both sides need to be the same. If you want to site a particular motif or part of the pattern on the other side of the shade this is the time to do it. As mentioned before, most tailored shades have a back and a front. It is therefore possible to have part of the design of a fabric on the front of the shade and another section on the back, giving two different looks if the shade is turned round.

Machine along the pencil marks, again starting about 4cm below and continuing about 4cm above the marks. It is a good idea, once you get to one end, to turn the fabric round and sew again along the same line for extra strength. (You don't need to use the tracing paper this time, unless the fabric is a jersey.)

Trim the side seams close (3mm or so, depending on the fraying tendency of the fabric). Do not cut anything off the top and bottom. Press the cover whilst it is inside out but don't press the seams open.

Remove the tape from the side struts.

Turn the outer cover the right way round and re-site back onto the frame, matching the side seams of the cover to where the struts were bound. Pin the cover to the top and bottom rings, making sure that the seams are level and run evenly along their side struts. To start with, it is a good idea to pin the cover where the seams are to sit on the top and bottom rings. If you look inside the shade at this stage you should find that the raw edge of one seam is sitting along one side of the strut and, on the other side, the seam should be running along the opposite side of the strut. On one side of the cover there will be pencil dots; these guide marks show where the cover should meet a strut. Initially it will look as though the cover isn't going to fit properly but continue pinning and stretching until the cover is completely taut and smooth. Siting the cover back onto the frame is a lengthy part of shade making, so don't be disheartened if it takes longer than you'd expected.

Although it doesn't matter in which direction you place the pins on the top ring, it is worth getting into the habit of placing the pins pointing upwards on the bottom ring. Large standard shades can be quite heavy and if they are left with the pins in, pointing downwards

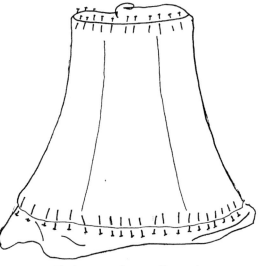

Insert the pins on the bottom ring facing upwards so they
can't be pushed out by the weight of the shade

Pin the cover on the top and bottom rings
until it is taut and smooth

and sitting on a work table for any length of time, the weight of the shade bears down and can push the pins out.

Over-sew using a lampshade stitch and a double thread for strength on the top and bottom rings, keeping the fabric taut whilst sewing round. This is why the excess handling fabric is not cut off at this stage; it gives something to hold on to, to keep the stretch. Sew along the outer edge of the ring rather than on the top of the ring. It is useful to have the frame in your lap rather than on a flat surface as you may need to angle the frame to sew it. You need to sew into the binding tape to secure the cover. This is a slow process as the double thread very often gets tangled on the remaining lills. If you try to force the needle through by pushing the end of the needle, you are likely to injure yourself as the eye end of a needle can still be quite sharp. A better technique is to 'work' the needle

in by pointing the tip of the needle in where you want to sew. Hold the needle between your thumb and fore-finger and middle finger and 'spiral' the needle in, in small circles, pushing as you go. It is kinder on your hands, has less potential for injury and the needle is less likely to snap.

Remove the lills as you go along; it makes the frame easier to handle and the thread less likely to get tangled.

Once you have sewn around the top and bottom rings, seal the stitches with a paper glue stick, by running the stick around the ring and smoothing the glue into the stitches with your finger. This simply stops the stitches from slipping, particularly if you have used a satin or more slippery fabric, but doesn't stop you sewing through it when sewing the lining in. Paper glue is ideal, as some stronger glues form a hard crust which is difficult to sew through.

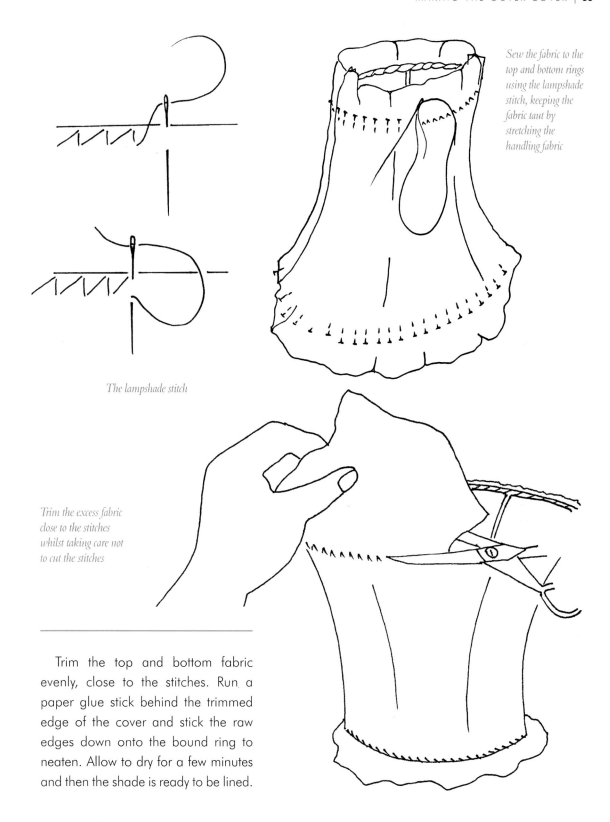

Sew the fabric to the top and bottom rings using the lampshade stitch, keeping the fabric taut by stretching the handling fabric

The lampshade stitch

Trim the excess fabric close to the stitches whilst taking care not to cut the stitches

Trim the top and bottom fabric evenly, close to the stitches. Run a paper glue stick behind the trimmed edge of the cover and stick the raw edges down onto the bound ring to neaten. Allow to dry for a few minutes and then the shade is ready to be lined.

CHAPTER TWELVE

Inserting a Balloon Lining

T*he frame is now covered with a tailored cover, the excess fabric trimmed and the edges neatened. If the intention is for the shade to be embellished, embroidered, beaded or appliquéd, this would be the time to do it, before the lining is inserted. The lining covers any stitching that would be on the inside of the shade after any embellishment has been attached and gives a clean, professional look.*

If you are sewing beads or sequins onto the shade they need to be sewn on individually. If you draw a thread from one bead to the next when attaching them, a 'spider's web' of threads shows when the shade is illuminated. This, of course, is not apparent when the shade is unlit.

Turn the covered frame upside down so that it is sitting on its top ring. Look down inside the shade and remove any loose threads from the seams or trim any slightly frayed edges and make sure that the loose ends of the binding tape are trimmed close. Anything that is left within the shade at this stage will show when the shade is lit so it needs to be really neat and tidy.

Take the lining and drop it into the inside of the shade, top side down over the fitting and gimbals, matching the 'wrong' side of the lining side seams to

the 'wrong' side of the side seams of the outer cover. All seams on a lampshade will throw a shadow when lit, so to minimize any extra shadows, the lining seam is put where the outer cover seam is, so only one shadow is seen. Pin carefully into place along the bottom ring (which is uppermost). Again you will have small dots on one side to help site the lining onto the place where the struts meet the ring. You will need a lill about every centimetre. These dots are, however, just a guide and should be used as such. The important thing is to keep the seam correctly placed in line with the tailored cover seam.

Once the lining is pinned all around the bottom ring, turn the frame over so that it is sitting on the bottom ring, pull the lining up to the top ring and pin into place as best as you can, trying to

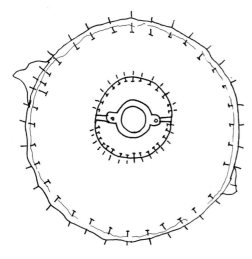

Look down inside the shade from the base to the top to see if the top ring has a symmetrical aperture

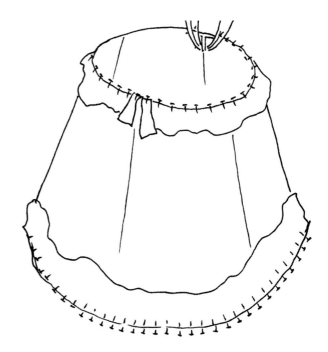

negotiate the gimbals. The lining will wrinkle around the gimbals so, in order to release this, snip down carefully where the wrinkle is with a small (sharp) pair of scissors, taking care not to cut the outer cover. It is best to do this a little at a time so that you don't cut down too much. This should release the wrinkle and the lining can be made neat around this area. Work the lining so that it is smooth and taut on the inside of the shade. The lining should ideally not touch the main fabric of the shade but just sit apart from it. To check whether the lining is stretched evenly, look down inside the shade from the base to the top ring and see if the aperture at the top ring looks symmetrical. If it is slightly lopsided then the lining has been stretched more on one side than the other, so needs adjusting.

When the lining fabric around the

Cover the raw edges, where the lining fabric has been released around the gimbals, with a small piece of satin ribbon. Pin into place

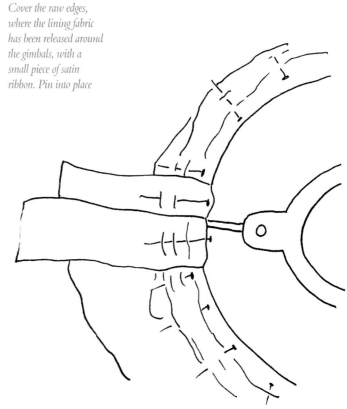

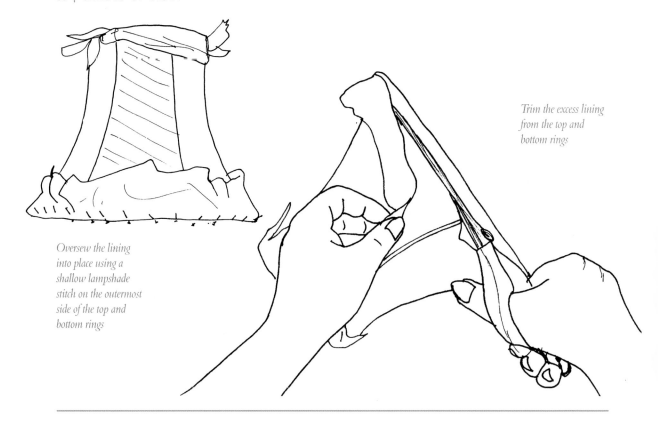

Oversew the lining into place using a shallow lampshade stitch on the outermost side of the top and bottom rings

Trim the excess lining from the top and bottom rings

gimbals is released it leaves two raw edges exposed. These are covered by a piece of cream satin ribbon as shown in the illustration on page 85 and pinned into place.

Although cream satin ribbon is the traditional way of covering the raw edge, a bias strip of the lining material will also work well, as would a narrow bias folded strip of the outer fabric.

Over-sew the lining, just over the outer edge of the frame, using a single thread matching the lining and using a shallow long lampshade stitch. Here it is not necessary to add the security stitch to every stitch; every third will be sufficient. Sew the ribbon in as you work your way around, treating it as an inte-

gral part of the lining. Siting the lining stitches on the outer side of the frame is important as this is where the trim will sit hiding the stitches. Any stitches elsewhere, particularly on the top side of the top ring, will be visible.

Once the lining has been sewn top and bottom, trim the lining close to the stitches. Unless you are using a satin or slippery lining there is no need to seal the stitches with a glue stick as jersey has quite a dry finish and will hold the stitches.

The shade is now lined and ready for trimming. This is both decorative and functional, its function being to hide the raw edge of the lining that is visible at the top and bottom ring.

CHAPTER THIRTEEN

Bias Trimming

Because most lampshades are based on a circular shape or involve some kind of curve, whether it is the rings or the struts, any trimming that is used to cover up stitches and embellish the top and bottom rings needs to be able to negotiate a curve of some sort. It needs to 'hug' into that curve and not stand proud of it. Lampshades have been traditionally trimmed with beading, scroll gimps and frills, but one of the most widely used trims is the self-bias trim. The self-bias trim is a band of bias binding made out of the same fabric as the body of the shade. It gives a clean, neat edge to the rings and, because it is made of the same fabric, blends into the shade. It is particularly effective where the focus of the shade is solely on its shape as there isn't any trim to detract from this, but it can also be used in conjunction with other trims – for example bead drops are often supplied on a functional ribbon, or frills on an elastic band, and a bias trim can be used on top of these ribbons or bands to hide them.

The main advantage of a bias trim is that, as it is made on the cross or bias, so it has an element of stretch and 'hugs' around the curved edges of a frame. Because of this tight fitting, it needs very little sewing to attach it to a ring. It is also used on the struts of a sectional shade to cover the stitches. Here, it can be used decoratively if made in a contrast colour, or functionally if made in the same fabric.

Method

Ideally on a self-healing cutting mat, fold the fabric diagonally at a 45-degree angle (so the warp threads lie against the weft threads).

Press the fold and cut along this line, ideally using a rotary cutter. Fabric doesn't like being cut on the cross and sometimes if scissors are used they produce a wave effect which is inaccurate and can cause problems with the trim later on. Using a rotary

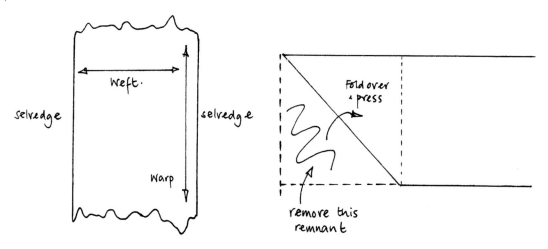

The bias-making process

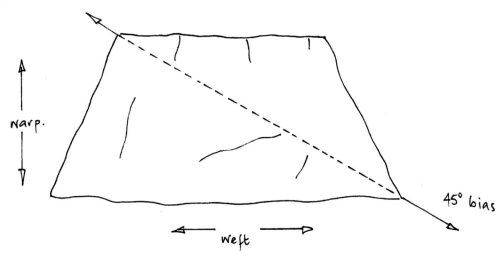

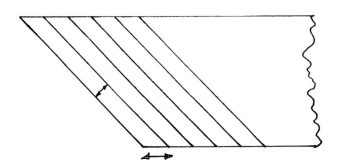

Width of strip measures less than the measurement along the selvedge because it is on the diagonal

Reed's School Photography Club

cutter gives an accurate, clean, true line. When using a rotary cutter always push forward and cut away from yourself to prevent injury. The blade needs quite a lot of pressure to cut the fabric; you will get to know the feeling of this as you practise.

Remove the remnant. The material is then on the bias or cross and is very stretchy.

Detail of chiffon pleated lilac shade, showing a bias trim covering the base ribbon of the beaded trim

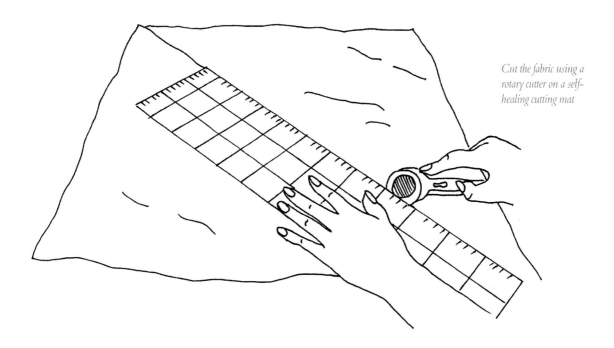

Cut the fabric using a rotary cutter on a self-healing cutting mat

Remove the remnant

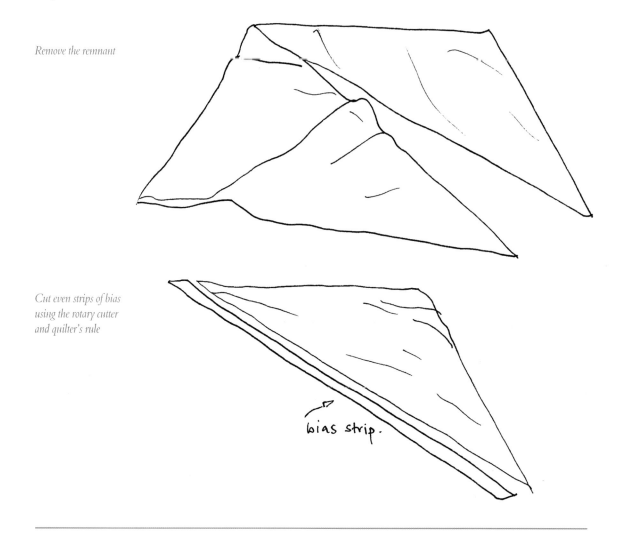

Cut even strips of bias using the rotary cutter and quilter's rule

bias strip.

Working from this bias line with a quilter's rule, decide how wide you would like the bias to be. (This may depend on the bias-making tool that you have.) Cut strips of the required width. If you are using scissors, then mark the fabric with a tailor's chalk pencil and cut carefully along the lines.

Remember that the width of the fabric strip will measure less than the measurement along the selvedge because on the selvedge it is on a diagonal.

Measure around the top and bottom rings of the finished shade (for very large shades it is easier to measure the diameter and multiply by 3.142 (π) to determine how much bias trim you need).

If you need to join bias strips together, all of the machining must be done on the straight of the grain to maintain the stretch and all the joins should run in the same direction. Place the two strips that need to be joined

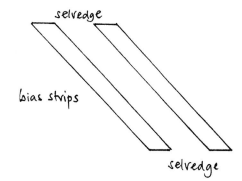

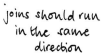

joins should run in the same direction

Joining bias strips correctly to maintain the stretch

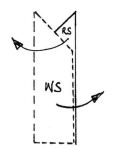

together 'right' sides facing. Hold the two shorter sides and turn so that the grain lines are together.

Move the strips horizontally to give the seam allowance. Pin and then machine from right angle to right angle. (You can backstitch this seam by hand, although a machine gives a better line.)

Press the seam open to embed the stitches and trim off the small triangles ('ears') of fabric that poke out from the side of the trim.

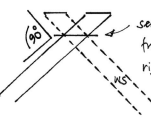

sew along this line from right angle to right angle.

The bias strip can then be passed through the bias-making tool and pressed to form the bias trim. The instructions given with the tool often suggest using a dry iron; however, I would be inclined to use a steam iron. This gives a crisper more durable fold, although care must be taken not to scorch the fabric. There is a 'knack' to using a bias-making tool: persevere with it and practise. It isn't an exact

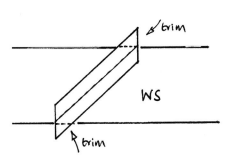

Thread the bias strip through the bias-making tool and press

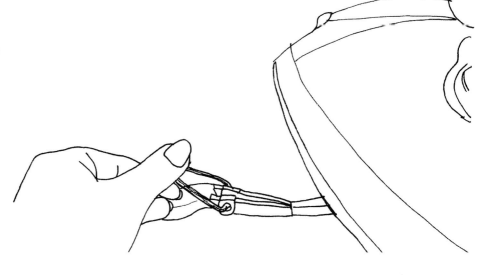

Turn the bias trim over and press on the right side

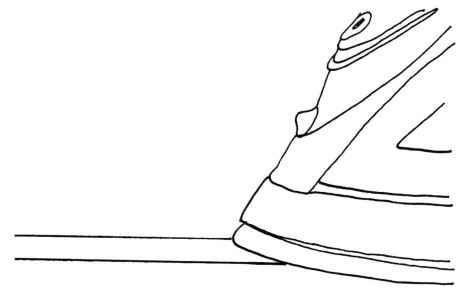

science so it is worth making plenty of bias trim and choosing the best bits. Remember to press the finished folded bias trim on the 'right' side as well in order to give a crisp finish. The resulting trim is neat and very stretchy and ready to be sited on the shade.

In order to site the bias trim onto the top or bottom ring, take a piece of bias and, with the 'right' side facing inwards, loop the trim around the ring and pinch together where it meets. The trim will be stretchy, so pull it in very slightly and put a pin through the join.

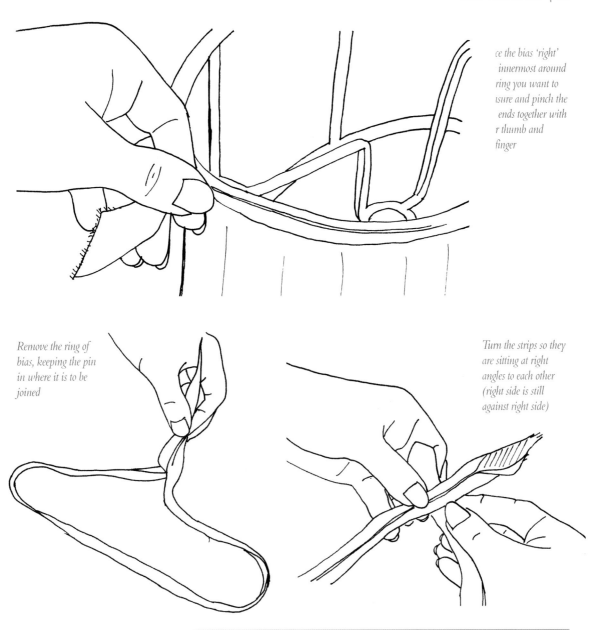

*ce the bias 'right'
innermost around
ring you want to
sure and pinch the
ends together with
r thumb and
finger*

*Remove the ring of
bias, keeping the pin
in where it is to be
joined*

*Turn the strips so they
are sitting at right
angles to each other
(right side is still
against right side)*

Remove the pinned bias trim ring from the shade and turn the point where it is to be joined so that the two strips are at right angles to one another. Unfold both of the strips at this point and pin from right angle to right angle ('right' sides are still against 'right' sides).

Machine along this line, press the seam open to embed the stitches, cut off the 'ears' and re-press the folds of the bias strip at the join to give a clean look. This diagonal seam is often almost invisible since the stitching follows the line of the weave.

*Unfold the folds in the
strips and pin
diagonally across*

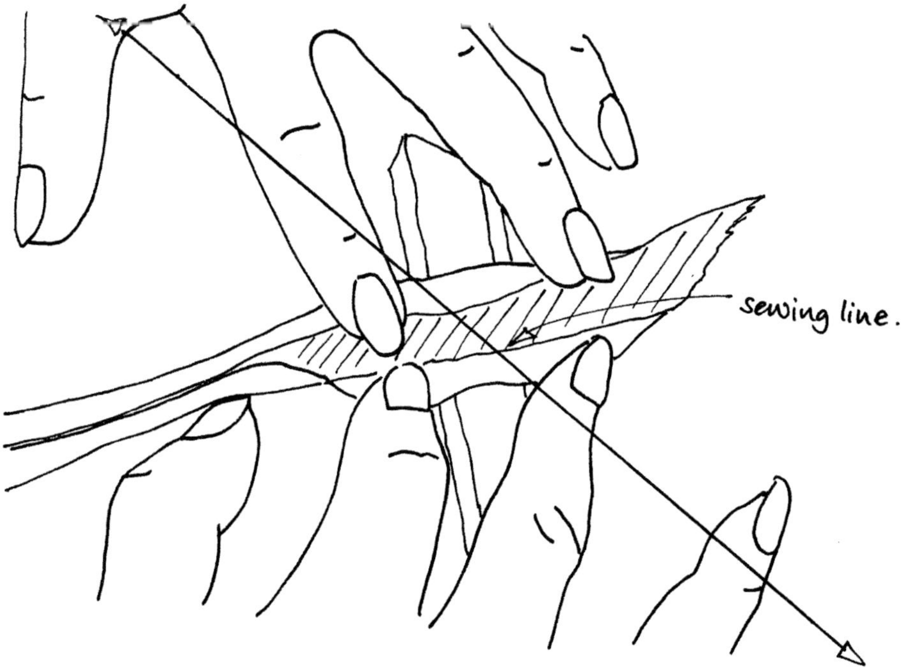

sewing line.

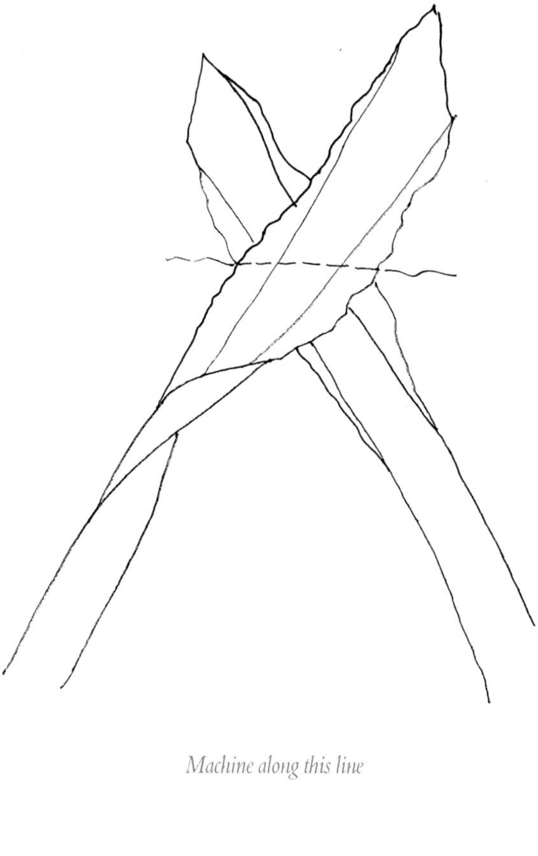

Machine along this line

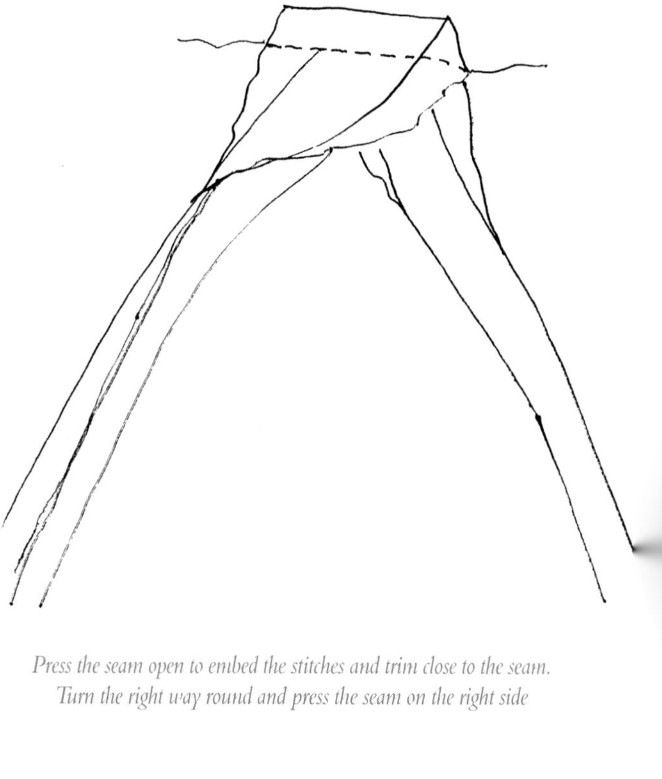

*Press the seam open to embed the stitches and trim close to the seam.
Turn the right way round and press the seam on the right side*

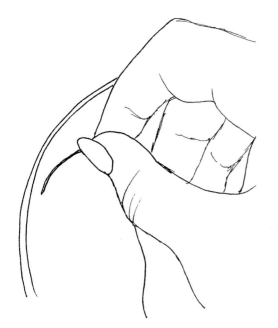

*Sew the bias onto the shade using
a scooping action with a curved needle*

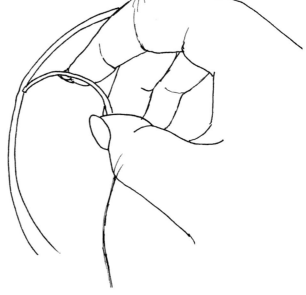

*The curved needle travels along inside the fold of the bias,
emerging after about 1 cm*

The joined ring can then be re-sited back onto the lampshade, matching the seam on the bias trim against a side seam of the body of the shade (so all the seams are in the same place). The bias ring should sit snugly on the shade.

If the bias ring is made accurately it needs little sewing to secure it; it really just needs keeping in place. Bias is best sewn on using a curved needle on the side of the bias that meets the lining.

Using a curved needle, hide the knot of the thread underneath the bias. Push the needle into the fold of the bias and 'scoop' the needle across inside the fold, allowing it to come out about 1 cm along. This scooping action is best done across a flat plane rather than scooping downwards. Pick up a few threads of lining and then scoop the needle back into the bias trim next to where the lining threads were caught. Again, run the needle inside the fold and allow it to re-emerge about 1 cm along the trim. The long stitch is hidden inside the fold of the bias, only emerging to catch a few threads of the lining to attach it to the shade. If you are not familiar with a curved needle, this technique may need a little practice. It is worth persevering though, as it is very difficult to sew bias on with a straight needle.

These stitches are virtually invisible, yet still hold the bias in place. There is usually no need to sew the bias on the

Reed's School Photography Club

Detail of bottom ring of Union Flag shade showing distressed bias on one edge only

top and bottom of the trim itself. Often sewing the bias at the bottom can cause drawn threads on the body of the shade itself, particularly on a plain shade. If the bias isn't sitting snugly against the body of the shade, this may be a measuring inaccuracy, but a way around this if it isn't too pronounced is to slip a small sliver of clear-drying glue up underneath the trim using a small strip of card and press down to neaten. (Don't use too much glue as it can show through the trim.)

Sew the bias on the opposite ring in the same way.

Bias made using a striped fabric makes a very effective diagonally striped bias (like a man's tie), as does checked fabric. Also, bias doesn't have to be folded on both sides. If just one side is pressed down, the opposite edge can be successfully 'distressed' to give a different type of edge.

Experiment with layering bias as an addition to other trims, or to cover functional bead ribbons or bands.

CHAPTER FOURTEEN

Trimmings

*I*t is often very difficult to buy suitable trimmings for your lampshade: decorative braids are sometimes difficult to colour-match, rarely made on the bias or able to negotiate curves and can be expensive, so it is helpful to know how to make a variety of trims in addition to the basic bias trim. A self-bias trim is usually used on the top ring whilst a more decorative trim is used on the bottom ring. The wider of the two trims tends to go on the bottom of a shade to keep the proportions correct. A handmade trim, whilst still being wide enough to cover the stitching on the ring, must be well made and accurate as it will be a feature of the shade. It can be made in the same fabric as the body of the shade, or in a complementary colour, and many trims can be made with velvet, satin or grosgrain ribbons; ribbons having the added advantage that their edges don't need to be neatened.

Ruffles and frills

A frill tends to be gathered down one edge of a strip of fabric, whereas a ruffle is gathered down the centre of the strip, creating a frill on both edges.

Decide how wide you would like the ruffle or frill to be and cut strips of fabric on the straight or bias to this width plus turnings. Ruffles require between two and three times their finished length of material, slightly less if cut on the bias and the edges can be neatened by hemming or zigzagging. These edges can also be left as a raw edge, frayed or pinked. One advantage of making frills or ruffles on the bias is that the edges can be distressed and frayed more successfully than when on the straight of the grain. Sew a line of running stitches along the middle or to one edge of the strip and pull up the gathers until it fits around the ring of the shade that you are trimming. Secure this gather by machine-sewing over the gathering stitch. Try experimenting with layering strips of the same width of fabric to make double ruffles and securing (with a small stitch or dot of glue) the outside edges of the inside strip at intervals. This gives a really full structural ruffle. Layer strips of different widths or colours for an interesting frill.

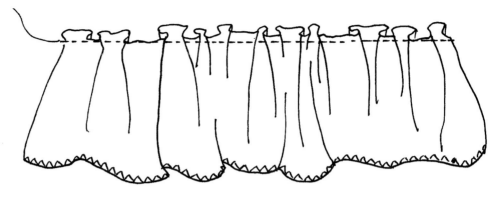

Single-edged frill

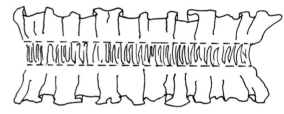

Wide ribbon centre ruffle

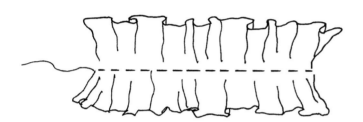

Centre ruffle

Ruched ruffle

RIBBON RUFFLES AND FRILLS

Use good quality ribbon and don't skimp on the quantities, otherwise it looks mean. The gathering stitching can either be done by hand or machine although gathered trims should be secured by machining. Try experimenting with layers of ribbon placed on top of each other. Double-sided satins and organza ribbons are best for ruffles and ruches as velvet and grosgrain ribbon tend to fold rather than ruche resulting in a concertina.

SINGLE-EDGED RIBBON FRILL

Secure the thread at one end of the ribbon and sew a line of running stitches lengthways along the edge of the ribbon. Gather the ribbon by pulling the thread and ruching the ribbon, easing the ruffles as you go to create an even ruche. Machine-sew along the hand-sewn running stitch to secure. By varying where the running stitch is sited on the ribbon, you can achieve many different looks.

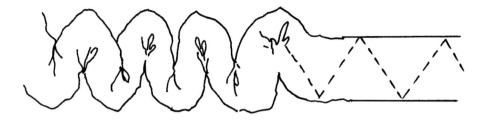

Shell edging made using a wide zigzag gather

Knife pleat trim

Shell edging

For this trimming a narrow length of tubing needs to be made, about twice the circumference of the ring you are to trim. The tube is turned 'right' side out and pressed with the seam running along the back of the tube. A gathering thread is then run in a wide zigzag, diagonally up and down as shown in the illustration above. Draw up the thread until it appears to lie flat throughout the length of the trim with equally spaced shells above and below.

This trim is also effective with double-sided satin ribbon and velvet.

Knife-pleated grosgrain top stitched

Because of its very structure, grosgrain lends itself to pleating rather than frilling. The pleats need to be measured accurately and tacked before machine-sewing to secure. A knife pleat is created by folding the fabric to one side in the same direction.

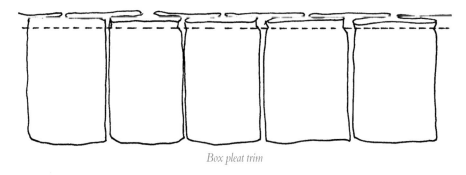

Box pleat trim

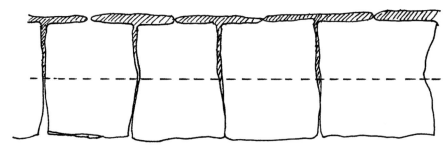

Box pleat, centre stitched

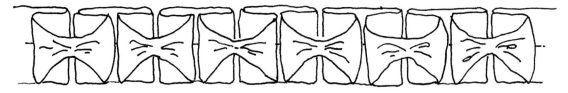

Tacked box pleats

Box pleats

TOP STITCHED

A box pleat is formed when two equal folds of fabric are folded *away* from each other in opposite directions. The folds meet evenly at the centre of the back. The pleats are secured by a machine stitch along one edge.

This is very effective in grosgrain and velvet as well as satin ribbons.

CENTRE STITCHED

As for top stitched, but with a line of decorative top stitching running along the length of the pleat on the centre line.

TACKED BOX PLEATS

Make these as for the centre stitched box pleats, then pinch the two outside edges together as shown in the illustration above and secure with a small stitch or bead.

CHAPTER FIFTEEN

Embellishments

O nce a tailored cover has been sewn onto the frame, this provides a taut base onto which embellishment can be sewn; it is rather like the fabric stretched within an embroidery hoop. Embellishments are surface ornamentation and are a good way of making a lampshade look unique. Surface embellishment has nothing to do with the trim that is sewn onto the top and bottom of the shade to cover the stitches, but is rather something that is added to the body of the shade for decoration. This embellishment, if applied carefully, can sometimes be removed to give a different look to the shade, but as with most decoration, less is usually more and it is a good idea to plan the design beforehand. Inspirations for embellishments can come from many disciplines, but millinery and fashion are two of the main ones. Owing to their size and shape, lampshades do have a look of hats about them so lend themselves to millinery-inspired embellishments such as feathers, bows and bands. Similarly, fashion embellishments can be used, as a lampshade shape sometimes echoes the shape of a dress or skirt. So, for example, corsages, buttons, and bows. The embellishment doesn't have to be permanent; pin badges and brooches are an ideal way of adding interest to a shade, and shades can be used as a vehicle for displaying a treasured piece of embroidery, a medal, a pin brooch, earrings, or similar. Embellishments can also hide a persistent wrinkle on a shade, or a mark that has occurred during the making process.

Types of embellishment

Embellishments can include the following items/techniques.

BEADS AND BEADING

Use tiny seed or bugle beads to ornament an existing fabric design, or use larger beads, pearls, crystals and even shells on plain shades to create texture and design.

BOWS

These are particularly useful on kitchen shades, but equally successful on shades which appear to have a 'waist'. Use different widths of velvet, organdie, taffeta or satin ribbons to create traditional bows and vary the length of the trailing ribbons. Wired ribbons allow for a structured bow, whereas a wide velvet or grosgrain lends itself to a flat Chanel bow. Whilst keeping within the style of the shade, try tying cords, raffia and even interesting string. These can, of course, be easily changed to create a completely different look.

BUCKLES

These can be made from leather, horn, coloured plastic, even diamante, and can be threaded with ribbon or a band made of the same material as the body of the shade. They also accentuate the 'waist' of a shade.

Duchesse silk satin tall asymmetric shade with diamante buckle embellishment, threaded with a self-sash

Reed's School Photography Club

BUTTONS

Use brightly coloured buttons and sew them on with contrasting coloured thread for a student's or child's shade; alternatively sew a collection of mother of pearl or shell buttons to a cream shade for a more feminine look.

ROULEAU

This is a decorative technique that involves creating patterns with self-piping, or cord. It is often used in millinery and dressmaking and is effective on a shade when made in the same fabric, as it creates lots of surface texture and detail when viewed close up and lit, but doesn't make the shade look too 'busy'. It needs to be sewn on carefully with a curved needle.

FEATHERS

These work very well as embellishment on a shade. They can be used in a small cluster at the side of a shade as would be seen on a hat, as a central fan, or as a trim around the bottom of a shade.

Stripped coque feathers, with a chevron cut or arrowhead, are dramatic in small clusters (always use an odd number). Marabou, which are actually braids of turkey feathers, are very soft and fluffy without a quill, and are available in lots of colours and widths. Pheasant feathers are available loose or on a braid and can be natural or dyed. And there are lots of other feathers to experiment with: ostrich and

Reed's School Photography Club

Scott Lewis Photography

Reed's School Photography Club

Scott Lewis Photography

Top left *Black silk shade embellished with a hair accessory corsage. As these can be clipped or pinned onto the shade they are easily removed or changed*

Top right *Silk petals from a deconstructed silk flower stab stitched into place. Tiny clear beads made from a hot glue gun give the impression of dew. (these are made separately and attached when cool)*

Bottom left
Freehand corsage created using a selection of ribbon types and widths whilst keeping to the same pink colour palate

Bottom right *Detail of broach corsage on a black silk shade*

emu feather fringing, turkey quills, pheasant tail feathers, etc.

CORSAGE, PETALS AND FLOWERS

Make self-corsages out of the fabric used for the main body of the shade, or utilize hair accessories, large fabric blossoms or corsages that are found in haberdashery departments. Try using felt to make simple flowers, or construct a freehand corsage using ribbons of different textures, widths and fabrics including wire ribbon to give some body to the structure. Crocheted and knitted corsages can also introduce texture and showcase another craft skill.

Detail of sequinned shade. Note: all of the stitches through the sequins must lie in the same direction

Scott Lewis Photography

Pleated drum shade showing dense sequinning around the base of the shade rising to sparser sequinning at the top, giving the impression of rising bubbles

Scott Lewis Photography

SEQUINS

These are flat, usually round, shiny discs with a hole for sewing and come in a huge array of colours and sizes, large sequins being called *paillettes*. They are effective on a shade in that they play with the light from the outside of the shade, even when it is unlit. They will draw attention to the shade so are not suitable for all settings and do have to be sewn on individually, which is very time-consuming.

ROSETTES

These can be either tiny fabric roses made by a swirl of fabric or ribbon, or the award type of rosette. The tiny roses in a cluster would give a cottage garden feel, whilst a single feature award rosette on a shade for a teenager can be effective.

Detail of linen self-swirl rosette

APPLIQUÉ

This term describes fabric cut-outs applied for decoration. These need to be sewn on very carefully using a stab stitch so as not to show the stitches. Appliqué ideas include re-siting a vintage section of embroidery onto a shade so it is illuminated from behind, lace and organdie appliqué panels, and children's decorative sew-on clothes patches and motifs.

HAND STITCHING AND EMBROIDERY

Use a matching thread to the shade to create a raised design that is only apparent when the shade is looked at closely, but which becomes very apparent when the shade is lit, or a delicate free hand embroidery with coloured threads as decoration. Be

Freehand rosette echoing the theme of the shade

aware of the back threads also being visible when the shade is lit, so it is best to keep lighting the shade as you are embellishing it.

POM-POMS AND BOBBLES

These are particularly effective on children's shades; they introduce an element of fun, texture and colour to the shade.

RHINESTONES

These are lustrous imitation stones made of glass, paste or gem quartz. They are sometimes in a 'cup' so can be sewn on through the ring on the back of the cup; sometimes they have a small hole or holes so you can sew through them, or alternatively they have to be glued on using a strong clear-drying glue.

BROOCHES AND BADGES

Use pin badges in clusters for a teenager's shade (always use an odd number and group together). Use the shade as a way of displaying diamante or ceramic brooches, hatpins, clip-on earrings and decorative birds. All of these things are removable so they can be changed with care. Other temporary decorations can include lace collars, as they are cut to fit around a curved shape, draping beaded garlands around the body of the shade, or even magnetized decorations.

OTHER IDEAS

Other ideas include cake decorations, silk butterflies, plastic toys and salvaged pieces. The important thing is to experiment, use other design and craft skills you may have and make the shade your own.

Attachment

When attaching these embellishments, ideally they need to be sewn on. This makes them secure and prevents glue seeping through the fabric to mark the shade. There is more control in placing the embellishment where you want it when sewing and, of course, if sewn on it can always be removed without damaging the shade if a different embellishment is required to update it.

Use a thread the same colour as the embellishment and use a small stab stitch to attach. Each stab stitch must be finished off individually as threads drawn from one stitch to the next may become visible as a 'spider's web' of stitches when the shade is lit. This is particularly important when beading, sequinning and embroidering.

A tailored shade stretched on a frame also provides an ideal canvas for silk painting *in situ* or for using fabric pens and stencils, but always test the fabric first for suitability.

CHAPTER SIXTEEN

Chiffon Ruche

*C*hiffon pleated and ruched shades are those where chiffon or a similar fabric is pleated or ruched over the top of a tailored cover. They have always been popular, but were particularly so in the 1950s. They have recently become fashionable again and can be found in London hairdressers and nightclubs. Chiffon pleated or ruched shades are particularly effective when lit, as the base colour shows through the chiffon pleating, so the choice of colour combinations of base fabric and overlaid chiffon is important.

There are two main options with this colour combination choice and it is worth experimenting. One is to have a strong colour for the base (an emerald green, for example) and ruche over the top with black chiffon. With this combination the shade will appear fairly black when unlit but, as soon as it is lit, the emerald green will shine through the black and give a dramatic effect. Alternatively, choose a base colour that is the same shade but a tone or two darker than the chiffon. Rather than giving a dramatic effect when lit, this gives depth to the shade and highlights the chiffon pleating or ruching.

Because the chiffon ruching becomes so apparent when lit, it is important to spend time getting the ruche right; choosing to have a ruche rather than a formal pleat gives a more relaxed look, but still requires an element of skill as it is still important to make sure there is no bunching of fabric and that the fabric is ruched evenly without looking too formal.

Either the whole shade can be covered with the ruching, or just certain panels, for example the four corner panels in a rectangular cut cornered shade. This can be a useful technique as the starting fold of the pleating or ruching will hide the stitching on the strut of the flat panel and the end fold will fold under to neaten the other side of the panel, avoiding the need to trim these side struts.

Fabrics ruched over the top of a base cover need to be sheer and soft and have good draping qualities. *Silk chiffon and georgette are ideal* (avoid organza, because, although sheer, it is

*Chiffon ruching on
individual panels*

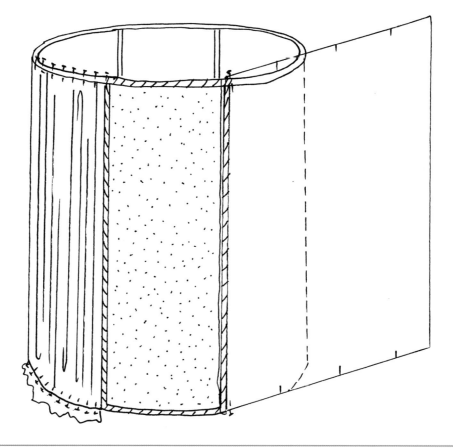

rather stiff). Chiffons and georgettes are available as synthetic fabrics; however they can be rather springy so silk is really ideal and kinder to your hands whilst working with the fabric.

Silk chiffons and georgettes are expensive fabrics and, because they are very fluid, they are difficult to cut in a straight line. Cutting with scissors or even a rotary cutter on a cutting mat invariably results in a very wavy line. In order to avoid wastage by incorrect cutting it is best to cut following a pulled thread. Lay the fabric on a work table with weft threads running from left to right and, with a pin or a needle,

attempt to hook up a single weft thread at the selvedge. This can be fiddly, so persevere. There is more likelihood of a warp thread being lifted, but this isn't what you want. Once you have lifted a weft thread, pull the thread through the fabric, and break it. This will then appear as a faint line running across the fabric from selvedge to selvedge, and, because it is one thread, will be an absolutely straight line across. You can then cut the fabric with sharp scissors following the line.

Another way of ensuring a straight line is to tear the fabric. Snip the selvedge with sharp scissors and then, with a firm grip, tear the fabric along the weft. This does, however, lead to two bruised edges and can sometimes damage the delicate fabric.

Method

Prepare and bind the frame, make the lining and put it to one side and sew the top cover into place. Do not, at this stage, trim the excess fabric from the top and bottom cover; leave the handling in place, and don't seal the stitches of the tailored cover with a glue stick. Any glue here will create a hard, crispy surface and make it more difficult to pin and sew into the base cover on the top or bottom ring.

Chiffon ruched shades require a lot of fabric. The ruching fabric is used on the frame in separate strips. Measure the depth of the frame and add between 8 and 10cm for handling: 4–5cm at the top and 4–5cm at the bottom. Ruching, and particularly pleating, usually runs down the selvedge grain of the fabric, although not always. Play around with the fabric before cutting to see which way it naturally wants to pleat; this usually becomes apparent quite quickly.

Cut the chiffon or georgette into strips of the depth of the fabric and, to estimate how much width of ruching fabric you will need, allow 2½–3 times the circumference of the bottom ring. The lower figure of 2½ will give a slightly sparser look to the ruche, although sometimes using a multiple of 3 can look too bulky. However, I would avoid using less than 2½ times as much, as the ruching can then look very mean. This is a glamorous-looking shade and skimping on the fabric will spoil the look. It is best to do a small test section to decide on the coverage needed.

Measure the distance between two of the struts on the bottom ring and multiply by either 2½ or 3, depending on the coverage that you want. If, for example, the distance between two of the struts is 10cm, the width of pleating fabric needed for this section is 30cm.

Mark out the strip of chiffon with pins or stickers showing where the struts should be. It is best to cut the selvedge off as it is usually slightly darker and thicker than the main body of the fabric and may show when pleated. The strips of fabric aren't joined; they are simply folded and slipped under or rolled over the last pleat of the previous strip.

Roll the first edge of the strip to incorporate any loose threads (these often only become apparent when the shade is lit) and pin to the top and bottom rings running alongside a strut (this ensures it is absolutely straight). Make sure there is the correct amount of handling above the top and bottom rings and then pin the strip of fabric where the marks are to their corresponding struts.

The fabric will hang in cowls all

Pin each section of fabric that has to fit into the space between the struts to ensure even ruching

section has been used and you have reached the next strut. The ruching is likely to need a little adjustment at this stage; there may be some small sections that need reworking – this is to be expected. There is a fine line between achieving a relaxed, pleasing ruched effect and an uneven bunched effect. It is also a good idea to shine a torch through the shade at this stage as any uneven areas will be very pronounced.

Continue with the next sections. When you run out of fabric, roll the edge of the next strip and pin underneath the last pleat; the join will then be lost. Try to do this at a strut as it gives a straight line to work from.

When all the shade is ruched, oversew the chiffon or georgette into place on the top and bottom rings using a double matching thread and the lampshade stitch. The ruched pleats need to be pulled tight to give a taut, even look. There are lots of layers of fabric to sew through at this stage so the stitches need to be close, secure and deep into the binding.

Trim the handling fabric close to the stitches and insert the lining in the usual way. Trim the top and bottom rings. This trim needs to be substantial enough to cover lots of layers of fabric, so bear this in mind when choosing a trim. These types of shades are, however, highly decorative and do lend themselves well to a heavier, more extravagant trim.

around the frame and this indicates how much fabric needs to be ruched into each section. This ensures an even look.

Begin ruching the rest of the strip of fabric by pinning it to the bottom ring and then pulling the fabric up to meet the top ring following the grain line of the fabric. If the grain line isn't followed, the ruches or pleats have a tendency to roll, giving an uneven look. Remember to put the pins on the bottom ring facing upwards, so that when the shade is put down on a surface, the pins aren't pushed out by the shade's weight. Continue until all of the fabric in the

CHAPTER SEVENTEEN

Swathed Ruche

This technique is one stage on from the straight ruched method. These shades need a little more experience, so it's worth practising the straight ruched shades first before you attempt a swathed one.

For this technique to be effective you need to use a bowed frame of some description, i.e. one with a 'waist'. This allows the ruched fabric to hug into the waist of the frame, defining the shape of the shade. You can, of course, swathe a straight-sided shade but you lose the effect of the swathing.

Method

Bind the frame, make the lining and put to one side. Make a plain tailored cover and stitch to the frame. Do not cut off the excess fabric at the top and bottom at this stage, or seal the stitches with the glue stick.

As mentioned in the previous chapter, ruched or pleated techniques require 2½–3 times the area being covered, so measure the circumference of the bottom ring and multiply by 3. This gives the width of fabric to cut. (This will have to be done in a few strips, as fabric is usually not wide enough.) The depth of the fabric is decided by measuring (with a soft tape measure to hug into the curves of the frame) from the bottom of a strut (see A on the diagram on page 112), then

Tall bowed empire showing full swathed ruche in silk chiffon

Reed's School Photography Club

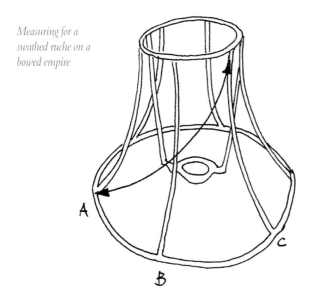

Measuring for a swathed ruche on a bowed empire

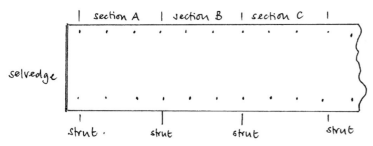

Mark the chiffon strips into sections as shown

Always start the ruching on the bottom ring

swathing the tape measure round to the top of the strut (see C), missing out one strut (see B). Add between 8 and 10cm handling to this measurement: 4–5cm for the top and 4–5cm for the bottom.

As with the straight ruched technique, mark out on the chiffon the area that needs to fit into each panel. It is often useful to mark in the handling allowance too.

The ruching always starts from the bottom ring. Remember to cut the selvedge off these strips and roll the first pleat.

Start to pin the strip into place on the bottom ring, beginning where a strut meets the bottom ring, allowing the handling at the bottom. Pin tiny pleats and ruches, fitting all of the fabric into the section of the ring. When the panel is finished on the bottom ring, take the markers that you have made on the top of the fabric and, instead of taking them straight up to its matching section on the top ring, swathe them up across the spare strut and start to pin them into place on the next corresponding section of the top ring, pulling the chiffon or georgette taut as you go along. The same amount of fabric has to fit into this top section, which is often smaller, so the ruching will usually overlap and the density of pleats will be more pronounced.

At this stage it is an idea to rearrange some of the pleats or ruches to get a pleasing effect, although it is unlikely to be right at the first attempt. Sew each

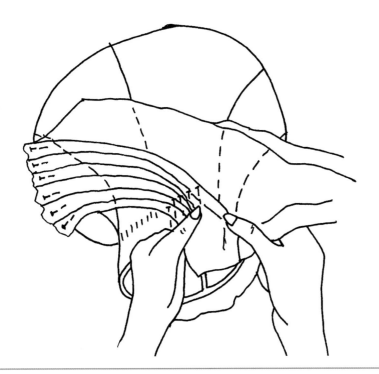

panel as you go, with the lampshade stitch on the top and bottom rings, leaving the first and last pleat pinned rather than sewn, so that the first pleat in the next section can be slipped underneath; this also makes the shade much easier to handle. When sewing, make sure that all the thickness of fabric is being secured into the binding – there are a lot of layers to sew through. Keep checking on the effect you are creating by shining a torch through the shade or illuminating it on a lamp base. This saves having to unpick sections that aren't right later on. The stage where only one or two panels are complete can look rather disappointing, but persevere, as once more of the panels are completed the shade begins to take shape.

Continue with each panel until the shade is completely covered. At the very last pleat, use a pair of large shears to cut the chiffon or georgette in a straight line; roll it, tuck this under the first pleat of the first panel and sew into place.

Trim the chiffon or georgette and the plain silk from the tailored cover together on both top and bottom rings; this gives a cleaner, more accurate edge as both fabrics are trimmed at the same time.

Insert the balloon lining and trim the top and bottom rings.

Reed's School Photography Club

Detail of chiffon swathed ruche. The close-up shows that the ruche is not formal, it is a relaxed gather

Suggestions

Instead of missing out one strut and swathing across two panels, experiment with swathing over different numbers of panels to give different effects.

As much as you are able, try to make sure any folds are facing downwards; this type of shade is a terrible dust trap, but downward folds minimize this slightly.

If you are making two shades (to go either side of a bed, or at opposite ends of a table, for example) then, as with the swathed sectional shades, decide whether you want the swathing to go in opposite directions to mirror each other, or in the same direction.

CHAPTER EIGHTEEN

Fan Pleating

This technique is really a variation on the chiffon ruching method. It is particularly effective on a straight-sided or fluted drum and is essentially a series of fan pleats worked in one direction and then in the opposite direction. As with all of these chiffon ruched shades, it is very effective when lit and, if the alternating inverted panels are in toning or contrasting colours, it also looks very pleasing when unlit.

Method

Prepare and bind the frame, make the lining and put to one side and sew the top cover into place. As before, don't cut off the base cover handling or seal the stitches with a glue stick. Decide how many panels of fans you would like to fit onto the frame. Mark on the frame where the sections of fans will go on the top and bottom rings. A separate piece of chiffon is used for each fan section and is stitched separately. Measure the dimensions of each 'fan'; this will be a triangular shape. Then, use the same measuring method as for the ruched shade described in the previous two chapters. The depth of the fabric to cut is the length of the long side of the triangle plus 8 to 10cm of handling. (A common mistake here is to cut the chiffon the same height as the frame, but the long side of the triangle is a greater length.) The width of the fabric to cut is 2½–3 times the measurement of the bottom of the triangle. Cut out all of the rectangular pieces used to make the fans before starting.

Starting with the bottom of the fan, roll the edge of the chiffon as before and pleat or ruche the fabric into the section marked on the ring, pinning as you go along. Then draw up the fabric to the opposite ring, pulling it into the tightest space possible. This forms the top or apex of the fan. The fabric will overlap considerably and be very tightly bunched in this top section, but try to make it look as even as possible. Because of the amount of fabric, it is a good idea to use dressmaking pins for this part, as lills are too short.

Stitch the pleats or ruches into place, leaving the first and last fold unstitched

*Measure the frame
and work out how
many fans are needed
as shown.*

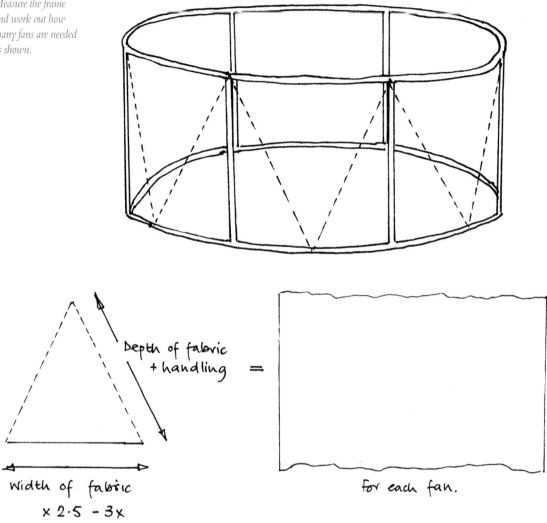

Depth of fabric
+ handling =

width of fabric
× 2·5 - 3×

for each fan.

so that the next fan can be slipped underneath. There are a lot of layers of fabric to go through, particularly at the apex of the fan, so make sure the stitches are small and close and they attach the fabric to the binding.

Turn the frame upside down and repeat, so the fan goes in the opposite direction, slipping the edge of the second section under the last fold of the previous one, thus hiding the join. Repeat until all the panels are covered. During the making, keep lighting the shade to make sure the ruching is even and pleasing.

Trim the chiffon and base handling fabric together. Line in the usual way and trim the top and bottom rings.

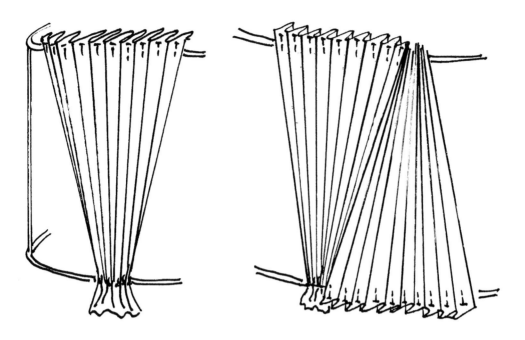

*Once one fan is in place, invert the shade and slip the first pleat
of the next fan under the last fold of the previous one*

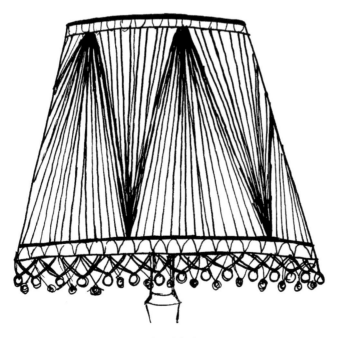

Fan pleated shade

CHAPTER NINETEEN

Sunray Pleating

The sunray or sunburst is a sheer decorative panel that is applied over the top of an existing covered panel. It is a design that was made popular in the Art Deco period and is very effective, particularly when lit. Several styles of frame are suitable for this as the sunray itself is usually over only one or two panels. However, it is best to avoid frames with concave panels as the finished shade shape is slightly altered by this sort of technique and won't look symmetrical unless all or opposite panels are used. Very small frames are also difficult as they are very fiddly to work on and sometimes the effect is lost on a small frame, so ideally a large, straight-sided shade for a standard or table lamp is a good choice.

As with the other ruching and pleating techniques the fabric used should be soft and sheer; chiffon or georgette are ideal. Ombre chiffon is very effective with this technique, especially if the darker section is gathered into the middle of the sunburst.

Method

Prepare and bind the frame as usual and make the lining. Choose the panel that you are going to make the sunray on and bind the side struts of this panel. You could also have two sunrays, one on each half of the shade, in which case the appropriate side struts should be bound accordingly. These stay on to give something to sew into, so need to be finished off and trimmed neatly. Cover the frame with a tailored cover, usually in a plain colour. Do not insert the lining at this stage.

On the chosen panel, decide where the centre of the sunburst is to be; this doesn't have to be central as shown in the illustrations opposite; the sunburst can fan out from the bottom of the shade or from one of the side struts. With a soft pencil, lightly mark on the tailored cover where the central point

SUNRAY PLEATING | 119

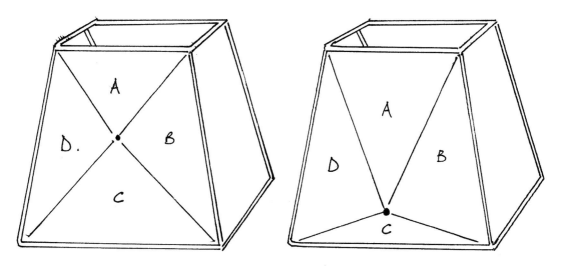

*Decide on the centre of the sunray and mark
on the tailored cover where the four sections are to be*

*The centre of the sunray can fan out from the bottom
of the shade. It doesn't have to be central*

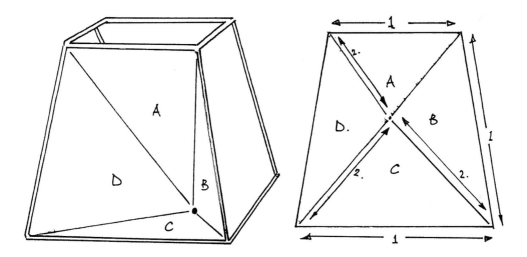

Another option for placing the sunray centre

Each triangle must be measured separately as shown

will be and then extrapolate four broken lines from this central point into the four corners of the panel. This panel is now divided into four sections and each piece is a triangular shape or fan. There are four pieces of material that go into making a sunray, essentially four fans, so the fabric is cut into rectangular sections as with the fan pleated technique. These four fans need to be labelled A, B, C, D and measured separately as they are often different (depending on the position of the central point).

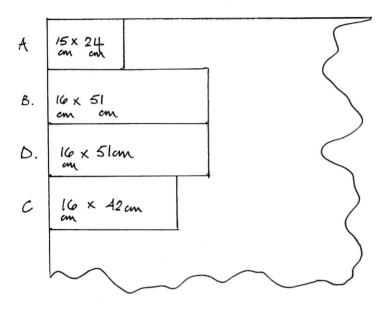

A   15 x 24
     cm   cm

B.   16 x 51
     cm   cm

D.   16 x 51cm
     cm

C   16 x 42 cm
     cm

Organize a cutting plan so as not to waste fabric

For example:

A Measure the outside edge of the triangle (e.g. 8cm) and x by 3 for fullness = 24cm.
Measure one side of the triangle (e.g. 10cm) and add 5cm* handling = 15cm.
You therefore need to cut a strip of fabric 24 x 15cm.

B (Often the same as D.) Measure the outside strut (e.g. 17cm) and x 3 = 51cm.
Measure the longest side of the triangle (e.g. 11cm + 5cm handling = 16cm).
You therefore need to cut a strip of fabric 51 x 16cm.

C Measure the outside edge of the triangle (e.g. 14cm x 3cm = 42cm). Measure the longest side of the triangle and add 5cm for the handling (e.g. 11cm + 5cm = 16cm). You therefore need a strip of fabric that measures 42cm x 16cm.

D The same as B on this occasion. Strip of fabric needed is 51cm x 16cm.

* There is a smaller handling allowance on sunray sections as handling is only required on one edge, not both.

When deciding on your cutting plan it is important to see which way the fabric naturally likes to pleat. Some fabrics have an obvious grain or 'crinkle' in the fabric, which shows which way it likes to be pleated but, as before, try pleating a piece in your fingers and it will be easier to pleat one particular way.

Put all of the rectangles of sheer fabric in alphabetical order in a line and, using a double thread or thicker goliath thread, sew a small running stitch along one edge using the smallest seam allowance possible. This technique used for gathering very thin materials such as chiffon or georgette is called fly running. Using a long, fine needle, take five or six small running stitches on the needle at once and push the material as it is gathered, off the needle towards the right hand, instead of drawing the needle out.

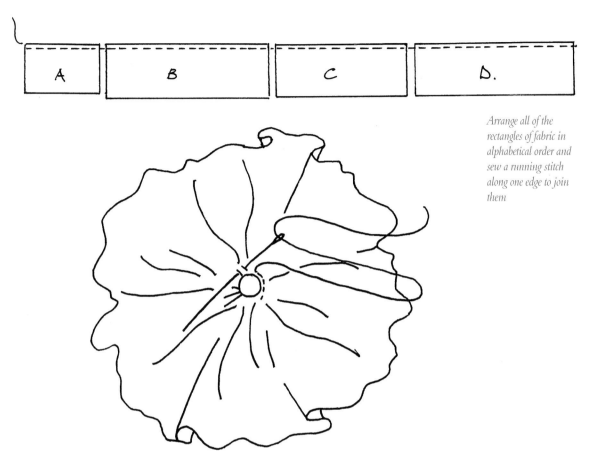

Arrange all of the rectangles of fabric in alphabetical order and sew a running stitch along one edge to join them

Pull the gathering thread up tight and secure

Move your hands a little further to the left-hand end of the material and repeat the process.

Pull the gathering thread up tight into a small, raw-edged circle and knot the thread to secure.

Sew this small circle very firmly into the centre of the chosen panel where the pencil mark is (or wherever on the panel you have decided the centre will be) and pull out the corners of the fabric to pin into the corners of the panel. Shuffle the fabric around so that it looks even (it is supposed to be gathered, not pleated). Roll the edges of the fabric pieces and slip the adjacent piece underneath so that there are no obvious gaps. Pin into place. You will be able to pin into the side struts, as you have bound these. Light the shade at this stage to make sure the effect is pleasing.

The reason why four separate pieces are used is to ensure even ruching

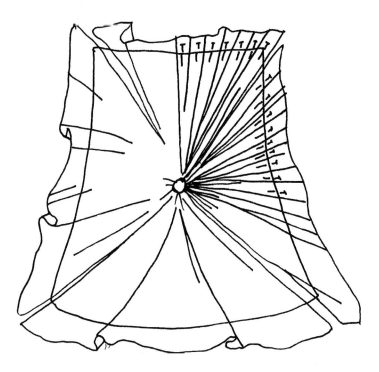

Site the centre of the gathered fabric onto the panel of the shade and fan out the four sections

around the sunburst. It *is* possible to use one long strip of sheer fabric but it is less accurate, wasteful of fabric and doesn't allow for different colours to be used on different sections of the sunburst.

Once you are happy with the ruching, using the lampshade stitch, over-sew the fabric into place all around the bound side struts and top and bottom rings and trim off the excess fabric close to the stitching.

The centre of the sunray has a lot of gathered exposed raw edges so this needs to be covered with a fairly substantial button or motif. There is a lot of bulk of fabric here, so whatever is placed here needs to be big enough to cover this area. A covered button in the fabric of the tailored cover is effective, or a large diamante button. A button with a shank is particularly useful as it can cope with the depth of fabric in this highly gathered section.

The side struts on the outer edge of the sunburst also have a row of stitches which need to be concealed. These can be covered with a self-bias trim or narrow decorative braid. This is usually glued into place as shown in the sectional shade technique in Chapter 22.

Line the shade with a balloon lining in the usual way and trim the top and bottom rings.

CHAPTER TWENTY

Knife Pleating

*P*leated shades have always been popular, particularly in a traditional setting. They do take time to do accurately, but can be done in stages. It's very important to keep lighting the shade whilst making a pleated shade, as one of the beauties of pleating is the pattern made by the layers of material in the pleats, which is accentuated by the light. This pattern therefore needs to be accurate and even to ensure it looks pleasing when back lit. This technique lends itself to straight-sided shades and can be used either all around the shade or on sections of a shade – for example, the cut corner panels of a rectangular shade. There are two techniques for knife pleating depending on the type of frame. First, pleating on true drums, where the top ring is the same circumference as the bottom ring and, secondly, pleating on empires where the top ring is smaller than the bottom ring. The latter is more challenging than the former.

Pleating on a straight-sided drum is straightforward because the pleat has to fit into the same space on the top ring as on the bottom ring. Pleating on an empire involves the same amount of pleats on the top and bottom rings, but those attached to the smaller ring (usually the top ring) have to fit into a much smaller space whilst still staying on the straight of grain.

Knife pleating is usually done in strips, which allows for different colours or tones to be introduced to give a different look. Test to see if the fabric you want to use is happy to hold a pleat by folding it and running your nail down the fold in the fabric to see if it forms a sharp crease. You will be unable to press in any pleats with an iron when the pleat is *in situ*, so it is important to check using this method. Fabric tends to prefer to pleat either along warp or weft, so turn your fabric to check which one is better. Silk dupion is ideal for pleating as it tends to hold a pleat well. Plain fabrics are usually best to use, as pleating a patterned fabric can have a tendency to look too 'busy' and you lose the look of sharp, clean lines of the pleat. Pleating has a one to three ratio, which means it uses three times the length of fabric of the section you are

Chiffon knife pleat overlaid on silk dupion base

pleating; it therefore uses a lot of fabric. However, the fabric is used on the straight of grain rather than the bias so there is little wastage.

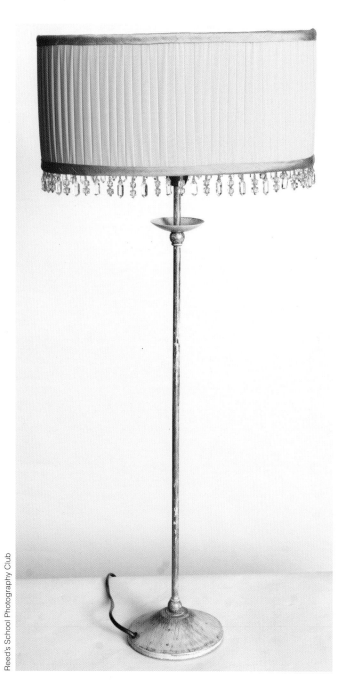

Knife pleating a true drum

First prepare and bind the frame, make the lining and put to one side. Remove the binding on the side struts where the lining template was made.

Measure the depth of the drum and add 6 to 8cm for handling. This is the depth of the fabric strips that you need to cut.

Measure three times the circumference of the bottom ring and allow an extra contingency of about 10cm. This gives the width of the fabric to cut, but as the fabric will probably not be wide enough, cut a few of these strips as long as the fabric will allow.

Measure from one strut to the next on the bottom ring and choose how wide you want the pleats to be and therefore how many will fit into the panel between two struts. For example, if the distance between the two struts is 24cm then eight pleats of 3cm each can be fitted in between each strut. As pleating requires three times the amount of fabric in each pleat, each of the eight pleats will require 9cm of fabric. The width of fabric needed will therefore be 8 (pleats) x 9 (cm of fabric) = 72cm width of fabric.

Mark the pleats off on the fabric at the top and bottom edges with a faint pencil dot, beginning with a pin 2.5cm in from the selvedge (which will be the first fold), then 9cm apart.

It is also a good idea to mark the edge of the frame with pencil dots on

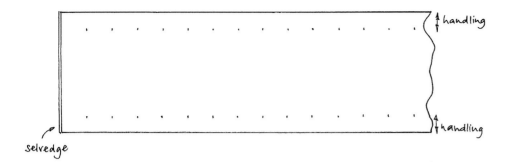

Mark the strips of fabric for the pleats as shown

the binding to show where the pleats should go. This, however, is only a guide as the pleating covers these binding marks, but occasionally they can be quite useful.

Take the first strip of fabric, 'right' side out, and pin in the turning width to the top and bottom rings (2.5cm) along a strut, exactly following the grain line. If the frame is small enough, this type of pleating is usually best done on your lap, holding the frame with your knees; this frees up both hands to do the pleating. (It is worth noting at this point that on most lampshades the pleats turn or point to the right.)

Hold the material in both hands between the thumb and first and second fingers and fold the fabric between the top and bottom marks you have made on the fabric. Pull the material taut along this line (which should be the straight of grain). Bring the fold over to lie (3cm) away from the first fold on the shade and pin into place bottom ring first, then top ring. On a straight-sided

frame the pleats will be the same at the top and the bottom. The handling should stay the same at the top and bottom if the pleats are straight. There must be the same number of pleats between panels (i.e. between one strut and the next). Remember to keep holding the shade over a light source as you go along to make sure the effect is even and pleasing.

Pleat each strip of fabric as shown

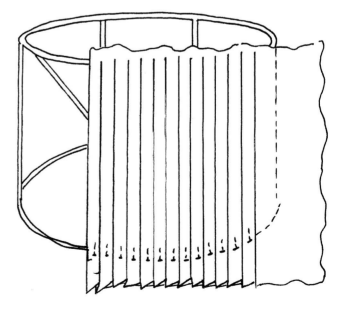

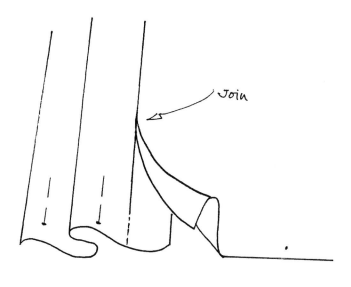

Join the next strip of fabric by folding it under the last pleat. The join then becomes hard to detect

The pleat must be on the straight of grain of the fabric, otherwise it will start to roll rather than have a sharp fold – and check that, when you reach each strut, the pleats are lying in a straight line along the strut. When you reach the end of the strip of fabric, join the next strip of fabric by folding it under the last pleat. The joins can be anywhere on the shade.

Continue until all of the frame is covered. When the last pleat has been pinned, trim the strip of fabric to about 2cm beyond the last fold and tuck this in behind the first pleat of the first panel. Go back and tighten up the pleats as much as possible by removing the pins, stretching and re-pinning, making sure each pleat is flat and taut whilst ensuring that the handling material is kept level at the top and bottom. This way you can make sure that the pleats

are not running off in one particular direction. A true pleat has three layers or sections to it and each of these needs to be held taut top and bottom, so the best technique is to use lots of pins very close together. Knife pleating requires more pins to be in place than any other lampshade making technique.

Before sewing the pleats into place, leave the first pleat just pinned to allow you to unpin it at the end and slip the last pleat underneath. Start sewing the bottom ring first, using the lampshade stitch and a double thread, removing the pins as you go. There are lots of layers of fabric to go through, so make the stitches close together for extra strength. Some shade makers like to stitch each section as they go, rather than sewing all at the end; this is a personal choice, but it is important to remember not to stitch the first and last pleats down of each section. Make sure you sew through all the thicknesses of materials and binding, otherwise the pleat will become loose. Cut the surplus material from the top and bottom rings close to the stitching. Line and trim as before.

VERSATILITY AND VARIATION

This knife pleating technique is very versatile; you can make the pleats whatever size you like and have as many or as few as you like in each section. You can box pleat a section or have a plain section of fabric and then

Knife pleat on drum. Detail of knife pleated shade. The top and bottom rings are trimmed with a bias made from the base cover fabric

introduce a few pleats maybe along one side. Knife pleating can also be done successfully on the gallery or collar of larger standard shades. It allows for different colours to be used on the same shade and allows you to experiment with different lighting effects and patterns. These patterns are created when some areas of the shade are more heavily covered than others; the light doesn't show through so much in these areas, whereas plain sections allow more light to diffuse.

Other variations are to do with combinations of fabrics. You can overlap chiffon onto the strip of dupion and incorporate this into the pleat, i.e. pleat together as one piece of fabric. This gives a different effect again from pleating the chiffon over the top of the dupion independently and it is worth experimenting with different combinations of colours.

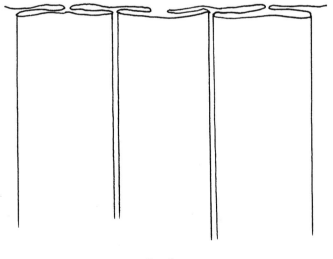

Box pleat

Rachel De Fraga Gomes

When the shade is illuminated the pleating becomes more apparent

Although, when learning, it is important to mark out the fabric to show where the pleats will be, when you become more experienced you may be able to pleat on a true drum by 'eye'; this is perfectly acceptable and often much quicker.

Knife pleating on an empire

On an empire frame the top ring is smaller than the bottom, yet the same number of pleats have to fit into the top ring as fit onto the bottom ring in each section. The folds on the top ring will

Scott Lewis Photography

Straight empire knife pleated in silk dupion

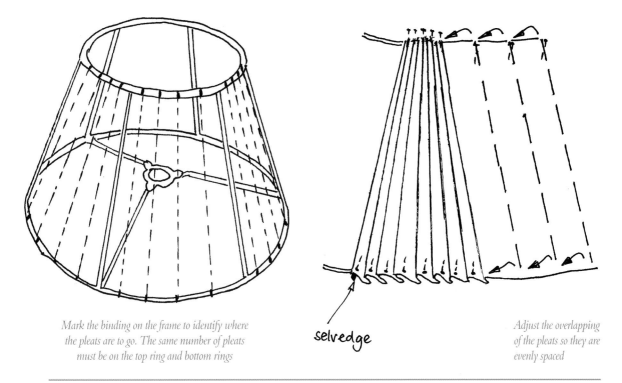

Mark the binding on the frame to identify where the pleats are to go. The same number of pleats must be on the top ring and bottom rings

selvedge

Adjust the overlapping of the pleats so they are evenly spaced

therefore have to overlap the previous pleat in order to fit in. There tends to be an excess of fabric on the smaller ring, which has to be tucked behind the pleats, and thus it doesn't look so tidy from the back. These shades therefore really do need to be balloon lined to hide this.

Mark out the fabric basically in the same way as for a true drum. However, when it comes to marking the actual binding on the frame to show where the pleats go, while you mark the bottom ring in the same way, because the top ring is smaller you need to divide the top ring by the number of pleats that are to fit in there and mark it accordingly. These guide marks will be closer together than those on the bottom ring.

Start as before by folding the fabric in on the straight of grain to give a clean fold, place along a side strut and pin into place. Always start with the pleat on the bottom ring and then pull up and pin to the top ring. These top pleats will have to overlap each other. Adjust the overlapping of the pleats at the top ring so they are evenly spaced. Do this with each individual pleat, so each pleat is completed as you go along. Check that, when you reach each strut, the pleats are lying in a straight line on the straight of grain.

Continue around the circumference of the shade, lighting the shade periodically and readjusting the pleats. Sew the pleats into place as before, line and trim.

*Shallow straight
empire knife pleated
in silk dupion and
hand-sequinned*

Other uses for knife pleats

Knife pleats are also very effective on a collared shade when they are bound tightly around the collar section. Make up the pleated shade as for a straight empire and sew into place. Then pull the pleats in round the collar section with a piece of narrow tape and secure. This gathers the pleats into the collar, allowing them to flare out further down the main body of the shade. Cover this tape with a decorative trim.

Knife pleats can also be swathed around a shade using the same technique as that for a swathed chiffon ruche. Very accurate pleating is required here, but the effect is striking.

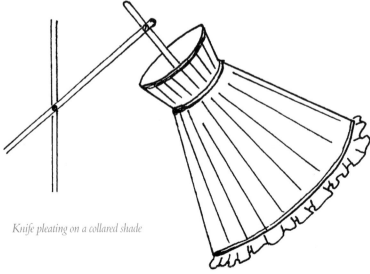

Knife pleating on a collared shade

Cheat Pleats

*C*heat pleats are not actually pleats at all; they are inserts which are added onto a finished shade and give the illusion of box pleats. They are quick and easy to do and have the added advantage of allowing you to insert a box pleat of a complementary fabric or contrasting fabric to give the shade some interest.

The shade is made up in the usual way with a tailored cover and the pleats attached before the lining is inserted.

Using a straight-sided empire or drum shade, decide how many pleats you would like on the shade, measure the height of the struts and decide how wide you would like the box pleat to be. Cut double this width plus seam allowances.

Place the 'right' sides together and machine along the long side; press the seam to embed the stitches and turn inside out to make a tube. Press the tube with the seam in the middle on one side, and repeat for all of the pleats. A pressed tube is made as it gives the pleat more body and prevents any raw edges being seen.

Pin the pleats onto the frame, hiding the seams at the back and arrange. Then sew the pleats into place onto the top and bottom rings. The pleats can be spaced apart or be close together

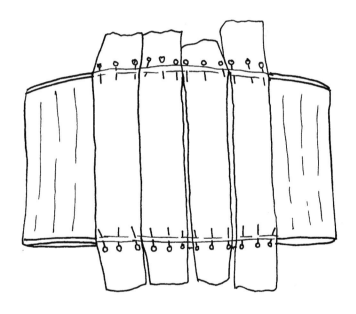

Pin the pleats onto the frame

depending on the look you want.

Once in place, the pleats can be pinched somewhere down their length and the pinch secured with a small stitch and bead to give a different look.

The pleats can also be made for a bowed shade. However, if placed in a vertical position, they will stand proud

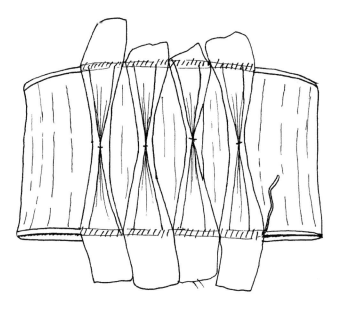

Pleats pinched in the middle of the strip

of the main body of the shade so it is best to twist the pleat around the shade, miss out a strut and attach to the top ring in the next section between two struts (as for the swathed ruched chiffon technique).

There are lots of design possibilities with this technique; perhaps consider using a striped pleat or a floral pleat in a complementary colour to the main body of the shade. Substantial ribbons, Petersham or velvet could also be used and a combination of different pinch points could give an interesting, almost smocked effect. Lots of cheat pleats overlapping can give the effect of knife pleating in small sections.

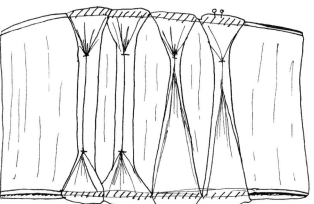

Pinching at various stages along the length of the pleat gives different effects

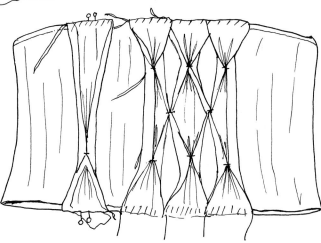

A smocking effect

CHAPTER TWENTY-TWO

Sectional Techniques

T his technique is used for square or sectional frames, unusual shapes such as petal-shaped frames and frames with a smaller waist than their top ring, like the corset frame. This method has to be used in this situation because a tailored cover, once made, would not slide over the top ring as the waist section would be too small to fit over. It is the method used for half shades and shields, or when working with a fabric that has little stretch. It is also ideal when you want to site a particular motif on the fabric in a specific place or direction on the frame, as each panel or section of fabric is sewn on separately. This is also the technique to use should you wish to have a different fabric on each different panel, or if a shade is to have corner inserts. It can be used for children's shades where a different colour is to be used on each panel, so it is a very versatile technique. There are, however, two downsides to this technique. The first is that the shade has to have a trim on each of the struts where the panel has been sewn. This can have a tendency to give it a cluttered look, as each panel is defined by the trim running around it. However, it can become a design feature if a contrasting trim is used. The best option if you want the trim to blend into the body of the shade is to use a self-bias trim.

Basic method

Prepare and bind the frame, top and bottom rings and opposite side struts, or the struts where the panel is going to be sewn on. On this occasion the side strut binding isn't temporary – it stays on for the life of the shade – so therefore needs to be tight and even and the knots over-sewn to secure, and trimmed closely.

Make up the lining in the usual way,
and put to one side.

Unlike the tailored shade, this time the outer fabric is used the 'right' side outermost. With the outer fabric on the straight or the cross grain (bias), place the fabric over the chosen panel of the frame. Start with a pin at each corner and then pin at about 1cm intervals on all four sides of the panel, removing the pins, reworking and stretching the fabric so that it is taut and free from wrinkles.

Sectional shade in gold silk dupion with large corsage embellishment

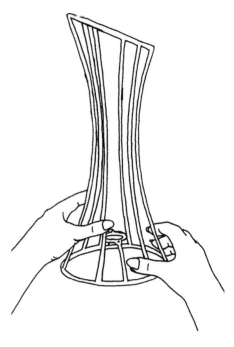

Decide which struts the panels are to be sewn onto

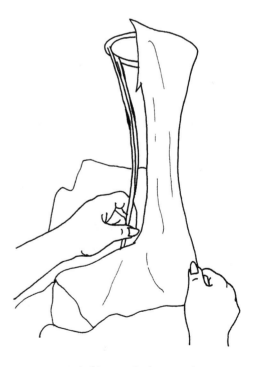

*Drape the fabric over the chosen panel
of the frame, right side outermost*

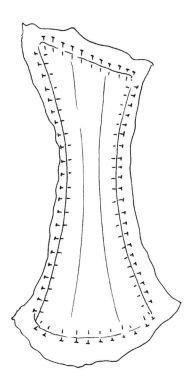

*Stretch and pin the fabric until it is taut
and smooth over the panel*

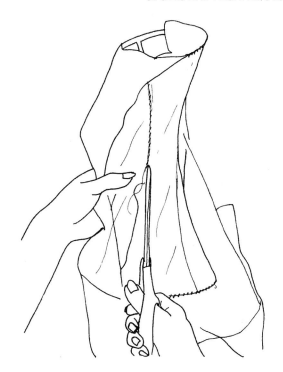

Trim the excess fabric close to the stitches

Stitch the panel securely to the bound struts with lampshade stitches, then seal the stitches with a paper glue stick and trim the excess fabric close to the stitching. This raw edge will eventually be covered by a trim so it is important to trim the raw edge close so that it doesn't extend beyond the edge of the trim.

Continue with the remaining panels.

Cover the lines of stitching and raw edges on the side struts with a decorative trim. Self-bias trim can be sewn on but is actually best attached by gluing as this is the neatest option. Use a clear-drying strong glue. With a small strip of folded cardboard or brush, pick up some glue either from the tube or

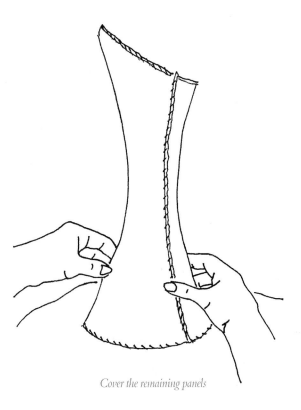

Cover the remaining panels

Using a strip of folded card, pick some glue up from a small tray or pot rather than using the glue straight from the tube. This gives you more control over where the glue is going

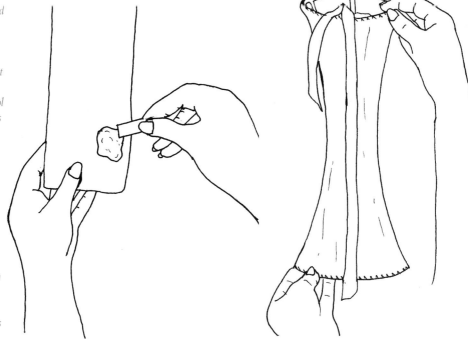

Site the bias strip

Detail of the side of a sectional shade. The self-bias covering the strut hides the stitches and raw edges

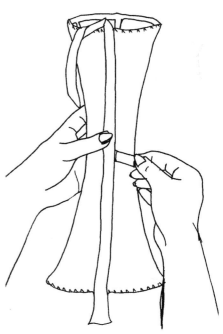

Using a folded strip of card, run a small amount of glue along the sides of the trim to make it lie flat

from a small pot and run a small strip down one of the struts.

Lightly press the bias strip along this; then it is sited in the right place. Be careful not to put too much glue on as this can seep through the trim and mark it.

Then, with the folded strip of card, run a sliver of glue up and down each side of the trim and press, almost pinch, into place on the strut; this secures the edges of the trim. Then trim the excess at the top and bottom of the shade.

Insert the lining as before and then trim the top and bottom rings in the usual way by hand-sewing into place.

Ruched sectional shade

This sectional technique doesn't need to have the fabric lying flat and taut; the fabric can be ruched on a panel or ideally from one side strut to its opposite strut, so that the shade is in two sections. This is particularly effective on a shade with a bowed strut, a bowed drum being particularly effective.

Prepare and bind the frame as for a sectional shade. With the fabric on the bias, pin the fabric ruching as you go (small uneven pleats) down one side strut, and pull these uneven folds diagonally across to the opposite bound side strut and bottom ring and pin. This will require a lot of removing pins and re-siting until you achieve your desired look. Ideally you will have any pleats or

Scott Lewis Photography

Black tightly ruched bowed drum made using the sectional technique

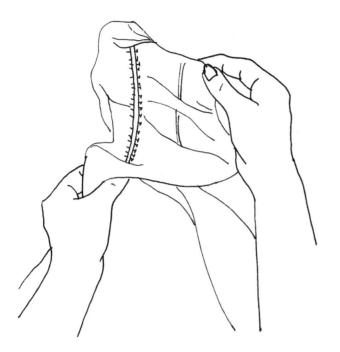

Ruche and pin the fabric down one side strut

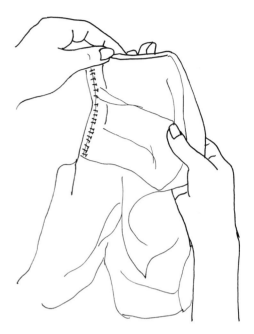

Pull the ruches over to the opposite side strut, arranging them as you go

Scott Lewis Photography

Close-up of ruched swathing on a sectional shade

folds facing downwards, otherwise they become dust traps.

The ruches can be very tight or quite loose depending on the look that you want. Sew the ruched panel into place and repeat on the opposite side. Trim the side struts with a bias trim or decorative trim. Bear in mind that, as there are folds of fabric on the side struts, this will be more bulky to trim neatly. If the ruches are not too tight they can be 'dressed' even after the panel has been sewn into place.

Lampshades often come in pairs, especially when used for bedside tables. When making ruched shades for such a situation it is important that you decide whether the angle of the ruche is to run in the same direction on both shades or whether the ruches are to run the opposite way.

Half shades and shields

Half shades or shields are usually found on wall sconces; instead of completely covering the bulb they simply shield it on one side only, with the exposed bulb facing the wall. They allow heat to escape more readily than other styles and, as they are not covered at the back, they emit a glow of light around the back of the shade against the wall.

These frames are covered using a sectional technique, so the fabric can be used on the straight of grain if required.

Bind all around the frame and place a piece of the fabric onto the front of the frame with the 'right' side outermost. Stretch and pin into place.

Sew all around the frame with the lampshade stitch to secure the fabric, seal the stitches with a glue stick and trim the excess fabric.

Take a piece of lining fabric and pin 'right' side outermost onto the back of the frame. Bring the edges of the lining over onto the front of the frame. Again, once it is stretched taut, stitch the lining into place on the front of the frame and trim away the excess fabric. As with inserting a balloon lining, you may need to snip around the gimbals to

Scott Lewis Photography

Large pink ruched shade made using the sectional technique, but with a relaxed ruche

release the fabric. These then need to be covered with a small piece of satin ribbon to cover the raw edges.

Using a self-bias or ready-made trim, glue or stitch a trim around the edges of the frame to hide the stitches.

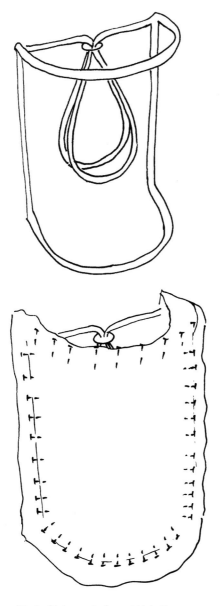

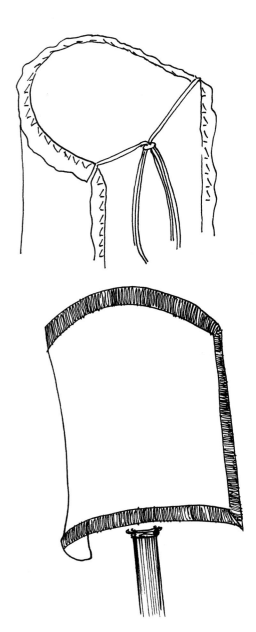

Pin the fabric onto the frame, 'right' side outermost

Sew the lining on the outermost side of the shade and cover these stitches with a decorative trim

CHAPTER TWENTY-THREE

Kitchen Shades

Unlike the tailored lampshade, which is fixed, a kitchen shade is a removable lampshade cover which was traditionally used in kitchens where it was necessary to wash shades frequently. They were often made in floral or checked fine cottons for this setting, or from utility fabrics such as linens or hopsack-type fabrics so they were easily laundered and suited the style of the room. However, when made in silks and other fabrics they can look much more sophisticated and be used in other areas of the home. They can also be used as slip covers for existing shades, perhaps for Christmas or a special party. They are relatively quick to make and use the fabric on the straight of the grain so there is little wastage. They are usually unlined, but can be made to be reversible so they then have a different-coloured lining. A kitchen shade requires a bowed empire, French or collared frame; these frames are used because they have a 'waist'. The kitchen shade is essentially a small bag which fits over the frame and is cinched in at the 'waist' or collar of the shade to give an empire line.

Method

MATERIALS REQUIRED

Frame

Fabric

Elastic (width dependent on size of shade)

Sewing machine

Tape

Large safety pin or bodkin

Sewing machine essentials (thread, scissors, tape measure, etc.)

Decorative ribbon

Small unlined kitchen shade on a collared Tiffany frame, made in duchesse silk satin and trimmed with black velvet ribbon and a diamante buckle

Reed's School Photography Club

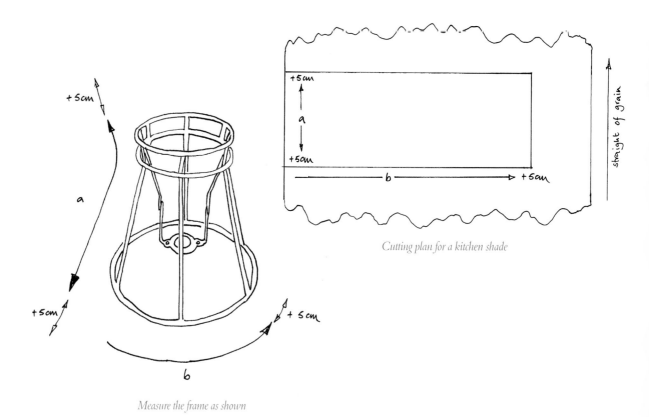

+5cm

a

+5cm

+5cm

b

Measure the frame as shown

+5cm

a

+5cm

b

+5cm

straight of grain

Cutting plan for a kitchen shade

PROCESS

First, there is no need to bind the frame. Measure from the top of the frame to the bottom with a soft tape measure, allowing the measure to fit into the waist.

For a medium-sized shade add on 10cm (4cm for the top, 4cm for the bottom, plus turnings). This is the depth of the fabric to cut (a). For larger shades a larger turning may be required to allow for thicker elastic.

Measure the circumference of the bottom ring (3.142 x diameter) and add 7cm. This is the width of the fabric to cut (b). This gives a soft gather;

should you wish to have a fuller gather on the shade you will need to experiment and increase the width of the fabric to cut.

Fold the material in half width-ways ('wrong' sides together) to form a circle and machine together with a very small seam allowance, e.g. 5mm. Do not press this seam open to embed the stitches. Trim this seam very close (taking care not to cut your stitches). Turn it inside out so the 'right' sides of the fabric are together and machine along the seam again with a wider seam allowance encasing the raw edge. This is a French seam and looks

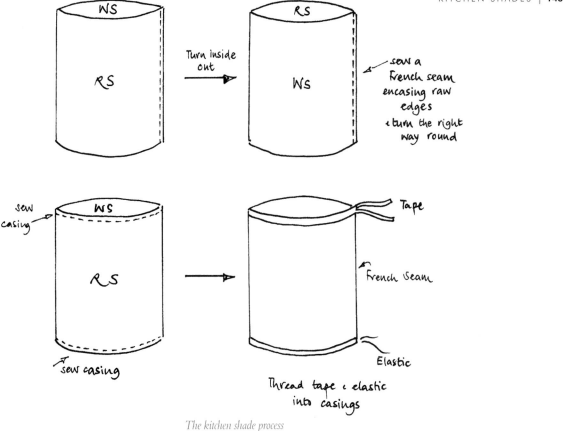

WS

RS

Turn inside out

RS

WS

sew a French seam encasing raw edges + turn the right way round

sew casing

WS

RS

sew casing

Tape

French seam

Elastic

Thread tape & elastic into casings

The kitchen shade process

neat on the inside as well as the outside. Turn out and press.

With the iron, turn and press in the raw edge and then make a casing at the top wide enough to take the tape you have chosen. Most table shades will use a 5mm width tape whereas a large standard shade may need something a little more robust, perhaps 10–15mm. Make another casing at the bottom wide enough to take the elastic. Machine these casings, leaving a small gap to insert the tape or elastic. It is helpful to avoid the seam area when deciding where to leave the small opening as this can cause bulkiness.

Thread the tape through the top casing with the bodkin or large safety pin and pull up loosely. Do the same in the bottom casing with the elastic. The elastic should be long enough when loosely stretched to fit around the bottom of the frame.

Slip the cover over the frame, the taped casing on the top ring. Draw up the tape tightly and adjust the elastic accordingly. Tie both the tape and elastic in tight knots and snip off the loose ends, tucking them into the casing. Dress the cover by arranging it into evenly spaced small gathers.

Put the cover onto the frame, tighten the tape and elastic and arrange the gathers

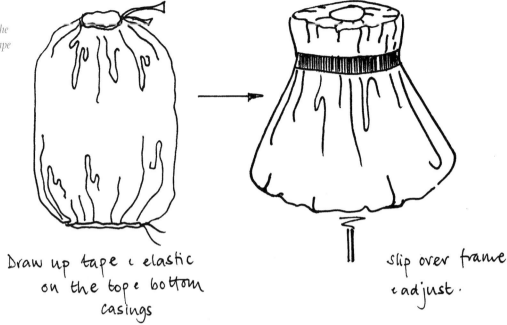

Draw up tape & elastic
on the top & bottom
casings

slip over frame
& adjust.

Cinch in the empire waist of the cover using ribbon or fabric, then tie and secure. Here you can use bows, buckles, knots, ties, brooches, and braids to embellish.

NOTES

- You can use elastic in the top and bottom rings if you so wish; this does make it easier to get the cover on and off easily.
- You may want to experiment with different widths of fabrics to give a fuller effect.
- Decorative bottom rings – particularly a floral or scalloped ring – are really effective with a kitchen shade.
- You can use fabrics not usually suitable for traditional tailored shade making, i.e. loosely woven linens,

embroidered fabrics, and also experiment with fabrics not normally used in soft furnishings – for example, wool suiting, shirting, tea towels, etc.

- You can turn a kitchen shade into a fixed shade by sewing a trim to the top and bottom rings (you will need to bind the rings beforehand so there is something to sew into).
- Kitchen shades are suitable for very large standard shades as well as small chandelier candle clip shades.
- It is possible to use a straight empire shade to give a different look. The cover is made up in exactly the same way but is not tied in at the waist. The shade has soft gathers all around it and is a useful cover for tired-looking empire card shades.

Detail of a kitchen shade

The 'waist' or 'neck' of the shade is cinched in with a velvet ribbon

Reversible kitchen shades

The reversible kitchen shade is one step on from the unlined kitchen shade. With a reversible shade you have two different looks within the same shade. So it is best not to use two patterned fabrics for the lining and outer covers as the different patterns will show through when the lamp is lit. The best

Vintage floral kitchen shade with complementary ribbon simply tied in a bow

option is to use one patterned and one plain fabric. Also, because there are now two layers of fabric and it is a gathered shade, this look is best used on a medium to large shade as it tends to look rather bulky on a smaller frame.

The materials required are the same as for an unlined kitchen shade apart from two complementary fabrics, one patterned, one plain. Ideally they need to be of a similar weight. It is also advisable to use elastic on the top and bottom channels as this makes it easier to get the cover on and off the frame to show the other side. Test the combination of the two fabrics by holding them up together against a light to make sure they are complementary before you start.

METHOD

Measure and cut the fabric as before; one for the outer and one for the inner sides of the shade. You need to be very accurate in making sure that both pieces are exactly the same size for this particular technique. On each piece of fabric, put the 'right 'sides together and machine-sew a seam with a regular seam allowance of approx 1cm. On the piece that you intend to use for the lining, initially leave a small gap of about 5cm halfway along the seam. Press the seams open to embed the stitches.

Put one of the 'tubes' inside the other and match the seams; 'right' sides of seams together.

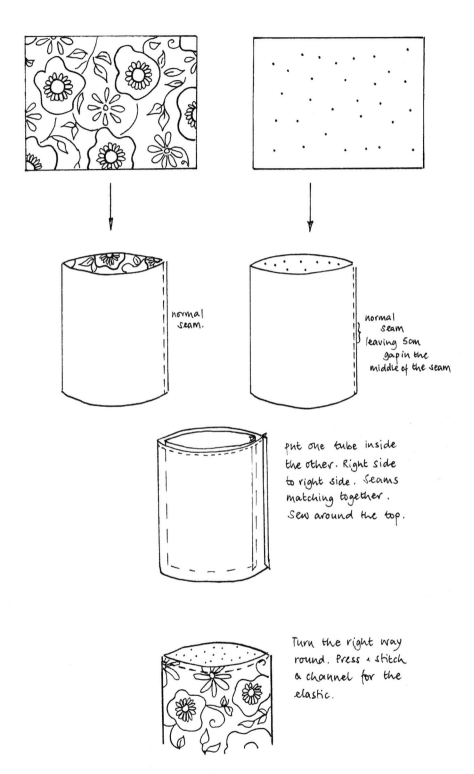

normal
seam.

normal
seam
leaving 5cm
gap in the
middle of the seam

Put one tube inside
the other. Right side
to right side. Seams
matching together.
Sew around the top.

Turn the right way
round. Press & stitch
a channel for the
elastic.

The reversible kitchen shade process

Sew around the top using a normal seam allowance, and then turn the right way so the 'right' sides are outermost, one tube is still inside the other, and press.

On the top of the shade, topstitch a channel for the elastic, this time starting at the seam, and leaving a small gap to insert the elastic at this seam point.

On the bottom of the 'tube' where the raw edges are, cut four evenly spaced notches into the inner and outer fabrics. Each corresponding pair of notches needs to be marked A, B, C and D, perhaps with a sticker on the 'right' side of the fabric.

Now you need to match the lining to the outer fabric *'right' side to 'right'*

side. Start with the seams and match the sides. Then start to match the 'right' side of notch A on the lining to the 'right' side of notch A on the outer fabric. This involves turning the bag almost inside out, looping it around on itself, finding its matching notch and pinning. Work your way around, matching the 'right' side of notch B lining to the 'right' side of notch B outer fabric and so on. The bag will turn inside itself a little as you work your way round. This can be very fiddly and instinctively feels wrong, but persevere.

Sew a regular seam with seam allowance. You will now have a small, twisted bag with the 'right' sides completely enclosed and 'wrong' sides outermost. It also appears to have the outer fabric on one side and the lining fabric on the other. This is correct.

Turn the 'right' side out again through the small gap that was left in the seam of the lining fabric.

Press and topstitch a channel for the bottom of the shade, again starting the sewing at the side seam so that it can be released to accept the elastic.

Ladder stitch the small gap left in the seam of the lining.

Thread elastic through the channels, place the shade on the frame and pull tight as before, securing the elastic and dressing the gathers.

Cinch in the waist with ribbon and the resulting cover will be totally reversible.

Match the lining notches to the outer fabric notches, 'right' side to 'right' side

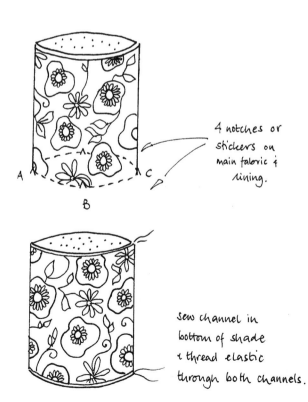

4 notches or stickers on main fabric & lining.

Sew channel in bottom of shade & thread elastic through both channels.

CHAPTER TWENTY-FOUR

Fabrics for Lampshade Making

*T*his chapter lists, and gives an explanation of, fabrics that are suitable for lampshade making. They are primarily natural fabrics (silks, cottons and linen) as these were the traditional materials used. However, as you become more experienced you will be able to gauge whether a fabric will work successfully and it is really worth experimenting with different fabrics to achieve different effects. Therefore, the list of fabrics in this chapter is not exhaustive, particularly when it comes to kitchen shades where most dress-weight fabrics can be used. It is worth experimenting with fine wool suiting, ticking, chambrays, poplins and linens to achieve different designs.

Explanation of technical terms

When describing fabrics, various technical terms are referred to. These relate to the manufacture of the fabric, as described below.

S AND Z TWIST

When threads are spun from their raw state they are twisted in one direction. This is either a Z twist (clockwise) or S twist (counter-clockwise).

PLY

The threads are then twisted together with more threads in the opposite direction from that in which they were originally spun to make a stable yarn; the ply of a thread refers to how many

Z and S twists

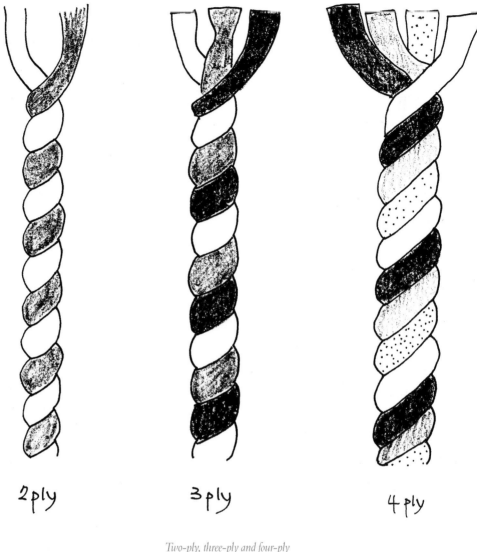

Two-ply, three-ply and four-ply

strands of these threads are twisted together to make it. The strength and evenness of a yarn depends on the number of plies.

THREAD COUNT

The thread count refers to the total number of threads, both weft and warp (see below), per square inch. The higher the thread count the better the quality of the fabric. However, thread count usually refers to cotton fabrics. Silk fabrics are measured in mommes (mm), which is a unit of weight to indicate their quality. Traditionally the weight in mommes was the weight in

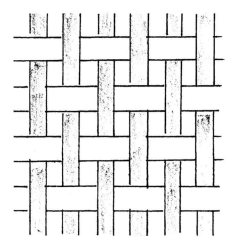

Plain weave

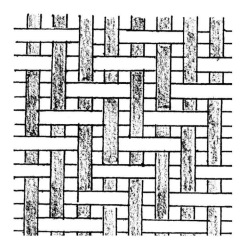

Twill weave

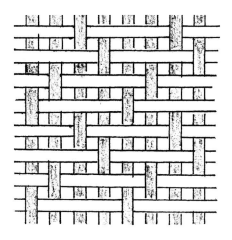

Satin weave

pounds of a piece of silk forty-five inches wide and a hundred yards long, but now it is measured in grams. A single momme equals 4.34g per square metre (gsm). So, for example, chiffon and georgette, being fine fabrics, are usually between 6 and 8mm, and dupions around 16mm.

WARP AND WEFT

The warp threads are those that run the length of the fabric and are attached to the loom; the weft or filling threads are those that run crossways, interweaving the warp threads. At the edge of the fabric the weft threads loop themselves back into the fabric and this creates the finished edge called the selvedge which doesn't fray, but is slightly tighter and therefore darker than the main body of the fabric.

FLOAT

A float is where the warp thread lies on top of the weft threads rather than being interlaced between them. These warp threads give a sheen to a woven fabric but have a tendency to 'catch' or snag easily.

Silks

Silk is a natural fibre; it is made from the cocoon that the silkworm spins round itself prior to emerging as a moth. The production of cultivated silk is known as sericulture. There are two main types of silk produced; mulberry silk derived from silkworms fed on mulberry leaves in order to produce fine silk, and tussah or wild silk which is taken from worms fed on oak leaves and is coarser, less even and, because of the tannin in the leaves, is mostly manufactured in natural colours.

In order to extract the silk fibres, the silk filament is unwound from the cocoon onto a reel, the filaments are 'bunched' into loosely twisted hanks, soaked to soften them and then dried. The filaments are rewound onto bobbins and then spun into yarn by a process called 'throwing'. The resulting silk yarn is then transferred onto larger cones for dyeing, weaving or knitting.

Silk is soft and luxurious, accepts dye readily, is strong, elastic, resilient, lustrous and resists mildew. All of these qualities are important in shade making, which is why silk is so widely used. However silk is weakened by the sun, marked by water and is expensive; factors which need to be taken into consideration.

There are a number of fabrics made from silk.

SILK DUPION

This is probably the most popular medium-weight silk, usually made in India. It is a fabric with an uneven surface and rough texture, made from yarns that are irregular in thickness. Dupion was originally the term used to describe the particular type of silk yarn that was spun from the silk of two cocoons that had nested together. The two silks were not separated in spinning and were therefore uneven.

Silk dupion takes dyes well so is available in a huge spectrum of colours and is easy to sew. Because of its matt textured surface it is very forgiving for a beginner as it doesn't highlight any small wrinkles and doesn't slip. It also takes creases very well so is ideal when making a pleated shade as the edges of the pleat have a really crisp finish.

Dupion is totally reversible, so is useful if the shade being made is unlined as the fabric looks the same on the outside and inside of the shade. It does, however, fray easily and as silk is a natural product it will always have a small amount of natural flaws. Black specks which occasionally appear in dupion silk fabric are part of the original cocoon of the silkworm. Removing them actually weakens the fabric, so they have to be accepted as part of its character.

SILK SHANTUNG

This is a medium-weight silk fabric woven with irregular yarns. The fabric has a dull appearance and rough texture. It differs from dupion in that, although it still has a fair amount of body, it is usually much thinner and has hardly any slubs. Any slubs it does have are small and narrow.

SILK TAFFETA

Silk taffeta has a crisp, firm texture with a fine-ribbed weave. The word 'taffeta' means 'twisted woven' and the material originated in thirteenth-century Persia. Taffeta is a plain woven fabric created by weaving a double thread in every other row and it is these raised threads rubbing together that create the swishing or rustling sound that is distinctive of taffeta.

Silk taffeta is considered to be a luxury fabric. There are two distinct types: piece-dyed and yarn-dyed. Piece-dyed taffeta can be used in lampshade linings and is quite soft. Yarn-dyed taffeta is much stiffer and has a lustrous sheen on both sides and is available in a variety of weights. The weight that is suitable for shade making can be rather stiff, so is not suitable for very curved frames and, because it has a sheen, it is unforgiving as every slight imperfection will show. For example, pin marks can sometimes show on taffeta, although they can be reduced by steaming.

FUJI SILK

Fuji silk is made from mulberry and tussah silk yarns that are spun, not wound. Because of this combination it is naturally a beige-coloured silk and is not available in a huge array of colours, but it has the advantage of being soft to the touch (it almost appears to have a nap) and is easy to sew.

SILK JACQUARD

Silk Jacquard is a medium-weight, luxurious patterned fabric, in which the design is incorporated into the weave instead of being printed or dyed on. It is made on a Jacquard loom which enables the raising of each *warp* thread independently of the others to produce a pattern. Because the design isn't printed onto the fabric, but is within it, it gives a fabric that is subtle when unlit and really comes to life when illuminated. The fabric has a good drape and is a good choice for shade making as long as care is taken not to catch some of the long weft floating threads. These snags become apparent when the shade is lit.

CRÉPE DE CHINE

This is a light, fine, plain woven silk fabric originally from China (the name being French: for 'crépe of China'). It has a good drape and a matt crépe finish. The crisp yet elastic structure is achieved by highly twisted S and Z twist threads alternating in the weft with a normally twisted warp thread. It is then woven from these hard-spun silk threads in its natural state and, when

Rachel De Fraga Gomes

Detail of overlaid pleated chiffon shade

woven, actually produces a fabric that is smooth and even, with no crépe-like appearance. The woven fabric is then boiled, which extracts the natural gum that is found in the fibres. During this process the weft loses its twist and the fabric becomes soft, causing the characteristic waved effect of a typical crépe de Chine. Although expensive, crépe de Chine is ideal for swathing and pleating over a tailored cover.

SILK CHIFFON

This is a loose, plain-weave, extremely sheer, diaphanous fabric with a gauze-like structure. Although it is sheer it is fairly strong and has a good drape. It is woven of tightly twisted crépe yarns in both warp and weft. Unlike in crépe de Chine, the weft yarn is *either* S *or* Z twist. The characteristic wrinkles in the finished fabric are created when the twist in the crépe yarn puckers the fabric slightly after weaving, giving it some stretch and a slightly dry handle.

Chiffon, because of its transparency, is most commonly used as an overlay in swathed, ruched and pleated shades. It is smoother and more lustrous than the similar fabric georgette, and is particularly effective in a changeant or shot form (see later) where the warp and weft threads are different colours. It can be very difficult to sew on a sewing machine because of its light and slippery nature, but when it is used in shade making as an overlay it is sewn by hand, so is ideal. Chiffon is also pinnable, as it will spring back, concealing any pin marks, but it is very difficult to cut accurately and does fray.

SILK JERSEY

This is a fine, lightweight knitted fabric. Like all jersey it has a lot of elasticity, which makes it ideal for lampshade linings; however, it is very expensive.

SILK GEORGETTE

A sheer, plain-weave fabric with a crépe appearance, this fabric is made like chiffon but uses a two- or three-ply yarn. It is woven with two very highly twisted S yarns and two highly twisted Z yarns alternately in both warp and weft. As a result it is a springy fabric with a matt finish. It doesn't crease easily, but like most diaphanous fabrics, it is difficult to cut as it is inclined to move, and it does fray readily. Having said this, it is easier to use than chiffon as it is slightly heavier and a little less slippery. As with chiffon and crépe de Chine it is used for a ruching and pleating overlay on a tailored base cover.

SILK DAMASK

A very old type of fabric first made of silk in Damascus, this is elaborately woven on a Jacquard loom, and has satin floats on a warp satin background. Most damask is self-toned; that is to say the warp and weft thread are in the same colour, and it is the design that creates the interest. As with other Jacquard fabrics, damask works well on a shade as long as the floats are not left to fray and the shade is not too curved, as damasks can sometimes be rather stiff and inflexible.

SILK NOIL

The word 'noil' actually refers to fibre length but is often used to refer to silk fabric made from short fibres. Silk noil is a rough, ivory silk from China. It is made from the short fibres from the cocoon rather than a continuous length of silk, so it has a rough texture and low sheen. Its main feature is that it has small pieces of cocoon woven into the fabric and these appear as dark cream flecks. It is easy to handle, sews easily, is relatively cheap and doesn't crease. It can, however, have a strong odour owing to the amount of impurities in the threads, so it is a good idea to wash the fabric before you stretch it over a frame. The heat from the bulb can also dissipate this odour, which is something to be aware of. It works for a tailored shade but is particularly suitable for a kitchen shade as it has a utilitarian look about it.

SILK SATIN

A very soft, lustrous, expensive fabric, satin is a weave that typically has a glossy surface and a dull back owing to the high number of weft floats on the fabric. It can be used for lampshade making, but is very slippery, snags easily and is unforgiving when stretched as it is so shiny, so not ideal for a beginner.

CRÉPE-BACKED SATIN

Crépe-backed satin is a heavyweight reversible two-faced fabric. One side of the fabric is satin and very shiny; the other side crépe, and dull. This dull surface is achieved by weaving with tightly twisted threads, alternating with an S and Z twist in the weft or filling direction. The advantage of crépe-backed satin in other disciplines is that both sides can be utilized, but in lamp-

shade making the crépe surface can often become a dust trap, so the shiny side is usually outermost. It is also a relatively inflexible fabric so care must be taken when choosing the frame shape.

DUCHESSE SILK SATIN

This is a thick, heavy, twill-weave stiff satin with a sophisticated sheen. Also called *'peau de soie'* meaning 'skin of silk', it is used mainly for wedding and evening dresses as it has a lot of structure to it, but looks stunning on a lampshade. It is, however, difficult to handle as it is fairly inflexible because it is constructed with a double weaving method using a high thread count, so

Pair of scarlet duchesse silk satin shades

Rachel De Fraga Gomes

Detail of duchesse silk satin shade with chiffon trim

it needs to be used on a shade without too many curves, or on a sectional shade. It has a tendency to 'roll' at the edges, when one is trying to lay it flat for cutting, is expensive and marks easily, particularly with any slight hint of grease. It is a dense fabric, so can be hard to hand-sew, and pins will leave marks. The fabric allows little light through it, so the light is thrown above and below the shade. This is a fabric to use when you have considerable experience.

SILK TWILL

This is a soft twill-weave silk fabric without much body, often printed. It is usually made up as scarves.

SILK BROCADE

This is a highly decorative heavy silk with a multi-coloured or self-coloured raised design, sometimes with metal threads added. Brocades are made on a Jacquard loom, usually in satin weave. In true brocade the design is produced by additional coloured threads in the weft. These pass across the back of the cloth unused and are brought back to the surface when required. These threads or floats make it easy to identify the 'wrong' side of the fabric.

Brocades fray easily because floats soon become detached when cut. Because brocades are made using a satin weave they can sometimes be slippery. They are best used on frames without too many curves as the fabric can be fairly inflexible. In addition to fraying easily, the large sections of floats held on the back of the fabric can throw ugly shadows, so it is best to line brocades with a heavy lining fabric so the light is thrown above and below the shade.

TUSSAH SILK

As explained at the start of this chapter, tussah silk is also known as wild silk and is produced in India by wild silk moths that feed on a wide range of vegetation, giving a variety of natural colours; most of the leaves they eat contain tannin, the substance in tea that leaves a stain in the cup. When the moths feed on oak leaves, for example, a honey colour is produced.

Wild silks are usually harvested after the moths have left the cocoons, cutting the threads in the process, so that there is not one long thread (whereas cultivated silkworms are killed before the pupae emerge, allowing the cocoon to be unravelled as one continuous thread). The threads produced therefore have an uneven slub, which gives a rough texture to the cloth and the resultant fabrics, usually made in a plain or hopsack-weave, tend to be thick and utilitarian looking. As a result of being both thick and of a loose weave these fabrics are often unsuitable for tailored covers, but work well when making kitchen shades for a more relaxed setting.

Shallow oval drum made in large botanical print chintz

HABOTAI SILK

Habotai is a soft, thin, light and slippery plain-weave silk with good draping qualities. This term actually means 'soft and light' and the silk was traditionally made in Northern China. It has insufficient weight or durability for the top cover of a shade, as it is not particularly hard-wearing, but is often used for the lining as it takes dyes well, so is available in lots of colours. Because of its smooth finish it is popular for silk painting and making scarves. It is an ideal fabric for making silk corsages as embellishment.

PONGEE SILK

A light silk fabric of slightly rough feel with excellent draping qualities, it is a plain-weave fabric and is sometimes used in lampshade linings.

CHANGEANT OR SHOT SILK

This is a silk with a two-tone, iridescent effect created by using one colour in the warp and a totally different colour in the weft of a fabric. A 'shot' is a single throw of the bobbin that carries the weft thread through the warp on the loom, but the term 'changeant' is also used, as the fabric does appear to change colour as it moves. Shot dupions and taffetas make interesting tailored covers and it is particularly effective when used in chiffon form on ruched and swathed lampshades.

MOIRÉ

This is a type of finish with a wavy watermark effect that can be applied to many fabrics but is mostly used on silk. The fabric is passed through engraved cylinders which press the watermark onto the fabric. When lit, the moiré pattern is highlighted, so it is a good choice for shade making. However, the calendering process by which the watermark effect is pressed into the fabric requires a silk that is fairly robust. This sometimes means that this type of silk is not particularly pliable for shade making on a frame with lots of curves.

Cotton and lawns

CHINTZ

Chintz is a good-quality glazed cotton fabric, usually with a large, colourful printed design of flowers, birds and fruit. It is a fine, closely woven cloth and only frays a little. It is suitable for shade making, although sometimes it is a little stiff because of the finish and high thread count. The glazing will wash off if machine-laundered, which may be a consideration. Also, the direction of any pattern needs to be taken into account if using chintz on the bias.

COTTON GINGHAM

A yarn-dyed plain-weave fabric, cotton gingham is a firm, hard-wearing cloth with checks woven in; white is always used with a colour. It is easy to handle and frays little, and is good for kitchen shades and attractive if parts are cut on the cross or to make bias trim.

EGYPTIAN COTTON

A fine, top-quality cotton originally from the Nile region, this is a plain-weave, soft cotton made into fabric which can be plain or printed. It dyes well and is strong and hard-wearing but soft to the touch. It is easy to sew and frays very little.

COTTON LAWN

A very fine, smooth, lightweight but hard-wearing plain or printed fabric, this is a plain-weave fabric made from cotton or linen, made famous by the Liberty Tana Lawn, printed with predominantly floral designs and Liberty's best-selling fabric. It was actually chosen by Liberty for its similarity to silk. It has a very fine thread count, which gives it a luxuriously light feel, and although very fine it is extremely durable. It is perfect for lampshade making.

COTTON POPLIN

A medium-weight fabric made from mercerized cotton yarns, this has a sheen and is often combined with polyester. It is available in plains and patterns and is very hard-wearing, and good for both tailored and kitchen shades.

SEA ISLAND COTTON

This is the best cotton yarn in the world. It is long, soft and smooth and is made into top-quality cotton fabrics, both plain and printed. Production is limited so it is a very expensive fabric.

CHAPTER TWENTY-FIVE

Stitches for Lampshade Making

T his chapter explains the different types of stitches that can be used for lampshade making.

Running stitch

This is a simple straight stitch and is used in lampshade making when making ruffles to trim a shade and sometimes when attaching braids and bought trims. The needle is inserted in and taken out of the fabric at evenly spaced intervals, thus the stitch on the back of the fabric is the same length as that on the front.

A variation on the running stitch is the tacking stitch, where the stitch itself is much longer. This makes it much easier to remove as it is a temporary stitch. It is used to hold fabric together before it is machine-sewn and is used in lampshade making to hold the four pieces of lining together when making the lining for a square or rectangular frame.

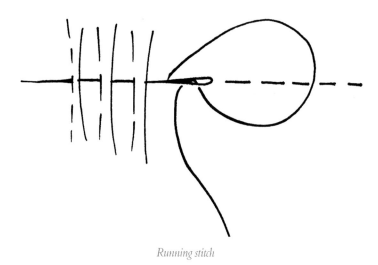

Running stitch

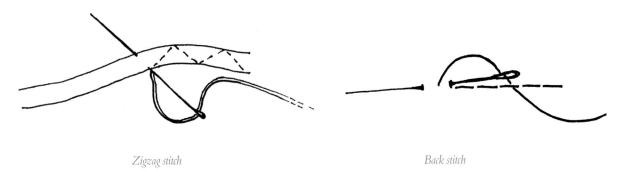

Zigzag stitch   *Back stitch*

ZIGZAG STITCH

This is a variation of the running stitch and particularly useful when sewing on bought trims that need attaching at the top and bottom of the braiding. Instead of the needle pointing in a straight direction it alternates up and down.

Back stitch

This is a strong stitch and is the hand stitch that is most similar to a machine stitch. In shade making it is used for sewing bias strips together if a machine is not available. Stitches are made in the opposite direction to the overall progression of the sewing. Starting with a running stitch, the needle is then inserted back down into the fabric at the end of the first stitch. The needle is then brought up through the fabric from the back a stitch space away from the previous stitch. Although this looks very neat from the front, it doesn't look particularly neat from the back.

Lampshade stitch

Although not officially called the lampshade stitch, this is the stitch that is most used during shade making. It is a very strong stitch which is secured at each stitch to prevent the fabric slipping. It

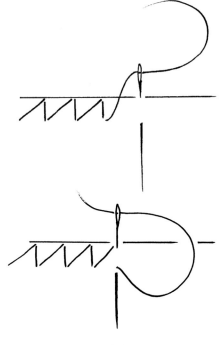

Lampshade stitch

Detail of pleated bias on the top ring of a shade. The pleats at the top are secured by tiny stab stitches, which are just visible in the photograph

has to keep fabric under tension for many years, so needs to be durable. It is a combination of a zigzag and back stitch and secures the fabric in both planes.

Stab stitch

This tiny, virtually invisible stitch is used in shade making to attach embellishments to the body of a shade. It is sometimes called an appliqué stitch. It is essentially a tiny running stitch in which the uppermost stitch is extremely short and looks like a little dot because

the needle is brought up from the 'wrong' side of the fabric, drawn through and then inserted back where the last stitch ended. The underside, back part of the stitch is long and runs to the next point of attachment.

Stab stitch

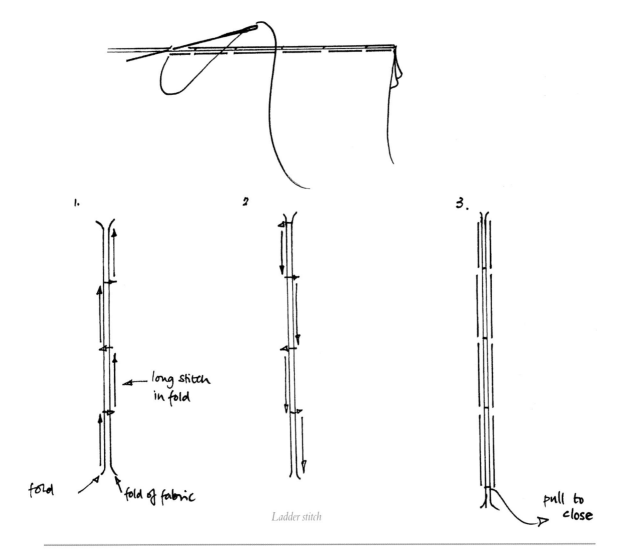

1.

2

3.

long stitch
in fold

fold   fold of fabric

Ladder stitch

pull to
close

Ladder stitch

The ladder stitch is a virtually invisible stitch used to close two folded edges. It is used when making reversible kitchen shades to sew up the small gap in the lining where the cover is pulled through and turned the right way round. It has the appearance of a ladder before it is pulled closed, hence its name. The needle is inserted into the fold of one side and the thread is run along inside the fold. The needle emerges further along the fold, crosses over the gap between the two folded edges and enters the opposite side. This is repeated until the end of the gap in the fabric. The process is then reversed and the stitches work down in the opposite direction. On reaching the beginning again, the threads are pulled taut, which closes the gap virtually invisibly.

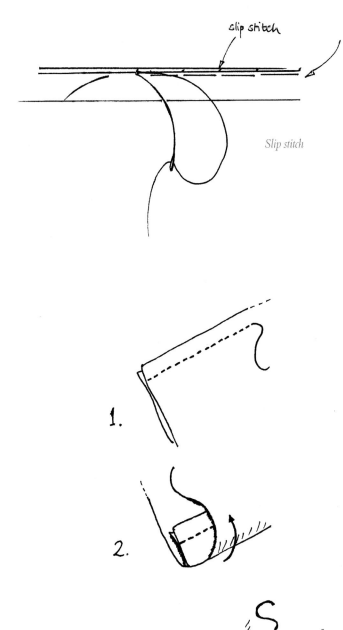

slip stitch

these long stitches are inside the fold

Slip stitch

1.

2.

3.

French seam

Slip stitch

In shade making the slip stitch is usually done with a curved needle when sewing the bias trim onto the shade. The curved needle scoops the thread inside the fold of the bias (so that it is unseen) then emerges from the bias to pick up a couple of threads of the lining, and then passes back into the fold of the bias. The section of the stitch inside the fold is a long thread, whereas the section picking up the threads on the body of the shade is very small. This makes for a virtually invisible attachment.

French seam

A French seam is one in which the raw edges of the seam are enclosed inside a fabric casing. It gives a very neat look and is used in kitchen shades where the inside of the shade may be seen. First, the two pieces of fabric are machined together with the 'wrong' sides facing. This seam is trimmed very close. The fabric is then turned over this seam so that the 'right' sides are facing and another seam sewn, with a slightly wider seam allowance to encase the raw edges.

CHAPTER TWENTY-SIX

Laundering Shades

If your shade is made using the traditional method (i.e. it is not glued anywhere) the fabric is colour-fast and the trims are sewn on (so it is possible to remove them if necessary), then it is possible to wash it. Ensure that your shade is made with a plastic-coated frame. If it isn't plastic-coated the frame may have a tendency to rust after it has been submerged in water. The important thing with washing shades is to rinse really well and then dry as quickly as possible to prevent watermarks.

Choose a hot, sunny, windy day!

- Remove any trim that is likely to bleed onto the body of the shade.
- Brush off any surplus dust, vacuum it, or use a sticky roll to remove dust.
- Using a hand-washing detergent, swish the shade around in a large bath of warm, soapy water. Rub lightly with a clean white flannel or cloth.
- Rinse well with lots of clean luke-warm water (a shower attachment is good for this) and shake out as much water as possible. When you remove it from the bath it will look rather saggy, but don't worry, this is to be expected. When the fabric dries it will tighten back onto the frame. With several clean white towels, blot out as much water as you can.
- Hang it on a washing line and dry as quickly as possible, or dry with a hairdryer.
- Ideally put it in a warm place (such as an airing cupboard) for the next twenty-four hours to ensure the fabric has tightened back onto the frame.
- Replace the trim.

CHAPTER TWENTY-SEVEN

Good Working Practice

Try to work in a clean, uncluttered work space. This space doesn't need to be very big, as lampshade making is a relatively light, portable craft. However, you may need to leave the shade and come back to it later, so the work space needs to be clean and ordered so your shade doesn't get spoiled. It is particularly important to clear up any stray threads. If they get between the lining and outer cover of a shade they won't be apparent until the shade is lit and that will be too late! In particular, clean and tidy your work space after you have finished a shade to start afresh: this prevents stray thread from fabrics contaminating the next shade.

Thread a number of needles in the correct colour of thread ready for sewing. Hand-sewing requires a rhythm which takes a while to get established during each sewing episode. To maintain this rhythm, it is easier to pick up a ready-threaded needle when you reach the end of your thread, rather than having to stop to re-thread every time, particularly with fine curved needles that are difficult and time-consuming to thread.

Make sure your scissors and any other blades you are using (e.g. rotary cutters) are sharp. Scissor sharpeners are available in haberdashery and hardware shops. Alternatively, take them to a knife sharpener or, for a quick fix, run a steel pin up and down the blade of the scissors. Remember, after sharpening any scissors, that it is important to clean the blades of any black residue before use, to ensure it doesn't transfer onto your fabric.

Ensure your sewing machine is in good working order and serviced. Your iron and ironing board must be clean.

Make sure your hands are clean; any grease or dirt can be transferred onto the shade, particularly with satin fabrics. Don't use hand cream just before making a shade; your fingers will be too slippery and may leave grease marks on the fabric.

Lampshade making requires an element of close, accurate work, so it helps if the work space is well lit. Natural light is always best, but daylight bulbs are very useful. Also, have a lamp base with a bulb available to light your shade quickly as you go along to check for stray threads, uneven ruching, etc.

Make sure you're comfortable. Everyone has a different style whether that is standing, sitting, holding the shade between your knees like a cello or working on a table. Find the way that is comfortable for you and relax your shoulders!

Don't attempt to pick up every last lill that you drop. It'll just waste time. Invest in a magnetic pin cushion and do a magnetic sweep at the end of the day to pick up any dropped pins.

If you drop the shade by accident, let it go, don't try to catch it. It'll probably be full of pins and you'll hurt yourself. Frames are fairly robust, so the shade will usually be fine.

Take regular breaks; walk away from the shade! However, when you leave it, cover your shade with a piece of fabric or a plastic bag. Unexpected things can happen when the shade is left; insects can leave marks, glue tubes explode, things can drop onto the shade. Believe me, it happens!

Throughout the process, be aware of health and safety issues. Only use products and materials that conform to your country's health and safety regulations.

Never exceed the recommended bulb wattage for the shade's size. Always use candle bulbs for small shade; pygmy bulbs are also available which are even smaller and make sure that the bulb and fabric never touch. Halogen light bulbs emit a lot of heat so are best avoided in a silk shade.

The most common causes of fire from a lamp are where the shade has been allowed to come into direct contact with the bulb, as a result of worn fittings and old or faulty wiring. Always have antique bases rewired if you are selling on to a third party.

CHAPTER TWENTY-EIGHT

Troubleshooting

- If you accidently prick your finger and get small blood spots on the shade, then take a piece of the straight frame tape and put some of your own saliva on it and then rub the blood spot with this piece of wet tape. The enzymes in your own saliva will break down the blood stain and remove it.

- If you need to wash a small spot on a lampshade, use distilled water (available in chemists); this is less likely to leave a water mark.

- If you have a persistent 'bubble' or wrinkle in the shade, as well as following the grain line (usually diagonally) and re-pinning the small section where this grain line meets the top and bottom rings, try turning the shade upside down to try different stretches.

- Sometimes silk can become overworked and stretched and persistent wrinkles will just not lie flat. In this situation, it is best to remove the cover completely and press with a steam iron. This steaming and subsequent drying helps to realign the threads back to their original position, so that another attempt can be made. Alternatively, hold the shade over a steaming kettle and allow the steam to release the fabric. As it dries it shrinks back onto the frame and this can sometimes resolve any overworking.

- Fingers can become very sore when shade making, particularly when pushing lills through fabric into binding and when sewing through fabric and binding. Try 'working' the pin into the fabric by wriggling it in almost a circular motion rather than simply pushing it in. When sewing, try to learn to grip the needle tightly between your thumb and forefinger and middle fingers and work the needle in by spiralling it in, rather than inserting the tip of the needle and then pushing it in from the eye end with the end of your finger.

- If you are having difficulty threading the needle, cut the thread at a slant, which gives it more of a pointed end to go through the eye of the needle.

- If your outer cover is fitting perfectly on one side but not on the other, it may be that your frame has been damaged and is not symmetrical. You may need to remove the cover and possibly the binding to realign the rings or struts.

Scott Lewis Photography

Bibliography

Barty-King, Hugh, *New Flame: How Gas Changed the Commercial, Domestic and Industrial Life of Britain* (Graphmitre, 1985)

Christopher, F. J., *Lampshade Making – Book Number Two* (Foyles Handbooks, London, 1953)

Dillon, Maureen, *Artificial Sunshine: A Social History of Domestic Lighting* (The National Trust, London, 2002)

Earle, Olive, *Lampshades – How To Make Them* (Dodd Mead and Company, New York, 1921)

Marsden, Josie A., *Lamps and Lighting* (Guinness Publishing, Middlesex, 1990)

Schivelbusch, W., *Disenchanted Night; the Industrialisation of Light in the Nineteenth Century*, trs. Angela Davis (Berg, New York and Hamburg, 1988)

Wray, Christopher, *Art Nouveau Lamps and Fixtures of James Hinks and Son* (Arch Cape Press, New York, 1989. Originally published in 1907 as *Electric Fittings, the Manufacture of James Hinks and Son Ltd*)

Vallance, Amyer, 'The Furnishing and Decoration of the House, VI – window blinds, lighting and accessories', p. 374 (*The Art Journal*, 1892)

Organizations

The National Trust
The Geffrye Museum

Index

WITHDRAWN

27.95   2/18/15